The Genius Project Manager

How Geniuses Can Know
What Others Can Not

THE GENIUS PROJECT MANAGER

Cover illustration design by Ignacio Huizar
Art direction by Guillermo Rodríguez

ISBN NUMBER: 978-1519745620

Dedications

For Frederick H. Munnell
Who Saved My Life

and for

My beloved wife Diana and daughters Sofia and Matilda, always with me and in my heart. My parents Rubén and Josefina, my siblings Rubén and Karla, my uncles Guillermo and Dina, my cousins Gunther and Memo for their unconditional love and support.

Table of Contents

Part III

Brief Research Reviews

These appear interspersed throughout the text.

1. Damasio, Antonio: "Descartes' **Error, Emotion, Reason and the Human Brain.**"
2. Schwartz, J. M. & Begley, Sharon, "**The Mind and the Brain, Neuroplasticity and the Power of Mental Force.**"
3. Nørretranders, Tor: "**The User Illusion, Cutting Consciousness Down to Size.**"
4. Lewis, Marc: "**The Biology of Desire, Why Addiction is Not a Disease.**"
5. Boyatzis, Richard: "**The Competent Manager, A Model for Effective Performance,**" and "**Primal Leadership**" (with D. Goleman & A. McKee)
6. Kuhn, Thomas S.: "**The Structure of Scientific Revolutions.**"
7. Greenspan & Shanker: "The **First Idea, How Symbols, Language, and Intelligence Evolved from our Primate Ancestors to Modern Humans**"
8. Sheldrake, Rupert: "A **New Science of Life**" and "**The Science Delusion**"

I

What is a Genius Project Manager?

What is a Genius?

A Genius is someone who knows how to access and use ideas, information and knowledge from their own insides. These are important because they make things possible that were otherwise *not* possible. Geniuses are unique because they consistently produce exceptional results. They see and know things others cannot see and do not know.

Geniuses speak a language that others do not. A Genius understands how reality functions with greater depth and power than what other people know. They use it to their benefit, for the benefit of their new ideas, and ultimately for everyone else's benefit.

Genius is the product of the deliberate, *knowing* interplay between waking consciousness and the non-conscious mind.

Geniuses generate new ideas and unprecedented solutions easily and regularly. This book will show you how they do this. Genius' results, in their area of expertise, far surpass those of others. Geniuses have a good time doing these things. They don't believe in "hard work," sacrifice or martyrdom. Life for Geniuses is the passionate creation of what they love. Ideas are their mainstay because Genius' ideas are not static. Neither are they.

Genius is never a fixed state. You don't "graduate" to Genius, then stop exercising it and forget about it. Geniuses chose to continuously become bigger than they have been before, based on their own standards. And then bigger than that.

For Genius project managers, their projects are life-sustaining in the passion and pleasure they provide. Genius project managers *know* things about their projects and their people that others do not. Genius project managers understand energy and its relationship to thinking and feeling. When there is a lack of energy they know how to remedy it. Genius project managers *easily* solve problems and generate innovative ideas.

If you don't believe this is possible, then you may think Genius is relegated only to music, like Mozart; or the arts, like Picasso; or for inventors, like Henry Ford; or for physicists like Einstein—absolutely unique individuals who were born to do what they did. You cannot know all that is Genius in the world, but you can know them by what they produce. Genius is possible in *any* realm of life and is available to *everyone*.

None of the conventional wisdom about Geniuses is true. Often, Geniuses are people whose desire for accomplishment was sparked by repeated failure and disparagement in early life. Something has sparked a massive desire in them.

Some Geniuses, in their treatment of other people including their own employees, seem to be real "jerks"— brusque, dictatorial and uncaring. Why is that? It's because although they have learned through experience to produce solutions and innovations, **they don't really know how they did it and get very angry when find they can't do it on demand**. Even the greatest Geniuses may not fully understand how Genius itself functions.

Geniuses are not a "commodity;" Geniuses are all unique. Each one is his/her own universe. So is every human being on the planet. It's not just the universe that is expanding; diversity in the universe is expanding beyond anything we can ever know. Geniuses manage to be themselves, the unique individual they really are, rather than the person their teachers, parents, friends or pastors told them they should be, and they stay faithful to themselves *above all else*.

Most people don't aspire to Genius, because they don't think it's possible for them to be a Genius at anything. That is also not true. A Genius is a creator, but a very focused and passionate one. We are all creators of many things, but Geniuses are uniquely focused on their creations and on their desires. There is no one else like them; that diversity is what makes Genius possible.

Most people assume that they have greater capacity than they actually use in their lives, especially greater *brain capacity*. People believe that there is a possibility that "if I only knew *how*, I could accomplish much more in life!" They just don't know how and they're not sure it's possible.

The mental hardware that makes it possible for you to be a Genius at what you do is already in place. It is your birthright. You wouldn't be a functioning human being if you didn't have it. You certainly have the desire. What it takes is a different perspective and a different approach about yourself and your circumstances.

Over time, if you are determined enough, that different approach may even physically change your brain, a process called brain *plasticity*; you've certainly heard that term thrown around these days. Once you know how Geniuses think, and especially when you learn their language, you won't be able to forget the new perspective. Being a Genius will just take a little practice. Most likely, many results will be immediate because much more knowledge about what's happening in your projects will become evident to you pretty quickly. The abilities Geniuses develop are never static; they expand and mutate in wonderful ways. Like any experience that gets a lot of practice, they also change the Genius' brain.

You will not see any of this material anywhere else. All existing material on project management is steeped in what we call *linear thinking*. With this material you will come to understand *non*-linear thinking, the unique language Geniuses use, but first we need to make sure you understand it's opposite. Then you will need to experiment, because your own language of Genius is unique.

All terminology and languages depend on understanding a contrasting idea, in order to understand any idea at all. If you don't know what *dark* is, then you can't understand *light*. If you don't understand what *mediocrity* is, then you can't understand what *Genius* is.

Linear thinking is used to train people in project management because projects, understandably, are considered *linear* processes. There is no graphic representation of projects that is not based on lines. That is good and absolutely necessary up to a point. Everyone needs to understand straight lines. Then again, who doesn't? However, the journey to outstanding results is *not* a question of getting better at understanding straight lines.

In the project manager job, **all forms of linear thinking are what the psychology of social motivation calls "*threshold* skills."** Threshold skills are defined and *required*, even *essential* for success on the job, but they, of themselves, cannot generate success or superior performance. In other words, *more is not better*. They are called *threshold* skills because they serve to get you in the door to the job. Without them, you won't get hired. *After that, however, the game changes.* Linearity will win you the job, but of itself, it won't make the project a win. You can't be a project manager if you don't understand project timelines, but being an expert at project timelines doesn't make your project a success.

Superior performance as a project manager requires *different* forms of thinking and acting. Did you think success meant just working harder, for more hours? That's a common misconception based on values people don't question, until they find themselves working very hard, not enjoying it, and producing mediocrity, while wondering "I'm a smart person; why is this happening?" This book is about passion, not drudgery!

All forms of education, training and certification in project management follow the same linear route. *More* of the particular activities, behaviors, skills and "knowledge" they espouse will not generate superior performance. Any training you receive will only enable you to get in the door and be hired for the job, but that's it. That's why...

- Being exceptional at managing budgets *won't* make you a better-performing project manager, or even better at staying on budget.

- Being superb at creating project plans, or using project management software, *won't* guarantee superior performance in the timely completion of those projects.

- Being a master at the technical content of your project *won't* improve meeting the requirements on that project.

- Being a master at code, being a superb writer, or being a software architecture master-mind—none of these will improve your performance as a project manager.

- Having many project management certificates and diplomas with superb results for your test performance can't guarantee the success of your projects. Those results are only evidence of your success at linear thinking.

So what *will* help guarantee success? What enable us to go beyond mediocrity?

First, there are two major obstacles you should be clear about before we continue.

This book is designed to give you the understanding you need to address them easily.

Obstacle number 1 is not knowing *how to think*, which is mainly understanding and appreciating the difference between linear and *non*-linear thinking.

You knew that a book about being a Genius was going to address thinking, something we are never, ever taught; not in school or anywhere else. We call it Genius thinking but only because the vast majority of people don't attempt it; no one has explained it to them.

It's counter-intuitive, but thinking like a Genius is really easy. Actual Geniuses simply are consistent about it and they keep track of their *thinking accomplishments*, because that helps them create more. They *like* to think, because of all that it produces. You'll like to think too, once you understand it and experience the knowledge it opens up for you.

There is a great difference between waking consciousness, which is the mental ability you are mainly using now, and the *non*-conscious mind. We'll explain these more and more as we progress because this difference is at the heart of how Geniuses operate.

Genius results are always the result of a deliberate, knowing interplay between waking consciousness and the non-conscious mind.

Geniuses think with *feeling*. That is the unique language they master. They understand that feeling is the language of their vast, non-conscious minds, while all other languages are linear and part of waking consciousness, which surprisingly, can't produce much.

Geniuses know how to consistently and deliberately use imagination, intuition, insight and introspection. These give Geniuses actual *knowledge*. Everything else is just *information*, no matter how much people may dress up their definitions to call the information on their servers "knowledge." It isn't. Knowledge is embedded in a human being.

Knowledge is *actively* held by a *knower*, not *passively* held by a *server*. Information is always *passive*. Knowledge is always *active*. That is their nature. Information, of itself, has no energy. People "pump it up," they forcibly "evangelize," but that takes effort, it isn't really fun, and it dries up. The right knowledge, however, is full of energy; it regenerates itself. It's the like the difference between numbers and passion, which is like the difference between dust and the universe.

Consider this: you went to school and learned to read. You learned math. You learned many other subjects and possibly went on to some form of degree-driven schooling at universities or other institutions, so you have diplomas. You may have studied for your employer. You learned a lot of content, but today, most learning is "vocational"—people want to know what you are going to *do* with it pretty early on. "What job are you preparing for?" Today, even children in elementary schools are asked, "what do you want to do/be when you grow up?" The acceptable answers are vocational ("I want to be a lawyer, doctor, butcher, baker, candle-stick maker," etc.)

Vocational schooling and education don't really have much to do with who you are, or even with what you aspire to. They provide *pre-defined categories* of activity that you assume an employer will give you money to carry out, as a job. The schooling for that job is filled with hierarchies of information. When you finish Schooling 101, you go on to Schooling 102. When you graduate, you get a certificate of some kind that is supposed to say you are reliably trained in, say, Basic Accounting.

All of these levels, titles, nomenclature, evaluations, certificates and diplomas are an indication of linear thinking and linear information. No real knowledge is involved. They call it "knowledge," but soon you'll see that it isn't. Information is a reproducible commodity; knowledge is unique and intimate to the knower. Information is in a book or in a server; knowledge is in a person.

In school, you didn't learn much about your brain and certainly not about *how to think*. That's because many people don't want you thinking on your own. You might begin to question what *they* believe and then they lose all control over what they want to control. Questioning, however, is a fundamental Genius process. **There is no schooling that will teach questioning—it goes against the principles of what schooling is about**. Schooling is about *not* questioning.

This book is not only about how to think, but also about the most essential part of thinking—although people don't think it is—which is *how to feel*. That's especially simple, because you can't help but feel. You are feeling something right now. Human beings are *feeling* "24/7"—it's unavoidable. What people *don't* believe about feeling is that feeling is useful and productive, and that feeling can be managed deliberately. People make themselves *victims* of feeling rather than *masters* of feeling.

What Geniuses accomplish isn't particularly complicated, but it is revolutionary, "counter-cultural," and usually disapproved of because it is so unusual. Einstein, Mozart,

Picasso and Henry Ford all had perfectly normal brains. They just knew how to use them and loved using them, although the people around them couldn't always appreciate what they were doing or how they were doing it. Have you ever heard anyone say, "stop day-dreaming and do something useful!"? Well, that can give you an idea of what we're talking about, which leads us to...

Obstacle number 2: paying attention to what other people think and say.

Most people, despite their best intentions, tend to produce mediocre results in their lives and in their work. Mediocrity is not what they want, but when they fail at getting what they want, they begin to create a mythology about life that says that life is exceedingly difficult and mysterious and dreams are a waste of time. That's only because they haven't figured it out. That isn't life at all.

When you have unreal beliefs, such as thinking that innovation is difficult; that people are impossible; that things never work out; that problem-solving requires analysis, and other such negative perspectives, then life becomes very much like those beliefs. This book is not, however, about "positive thinking," because positive thinking has little energy to it and alone, can't do the job. Without feeling there is no energy, no passion, and only poor results.

Some people have had such negative experiences and hold such negative beliefs with regard to money, work, careers, productivity and fulfillment, that they also believe that happiness is out of the question because, for them, the world is limited, rigid and constraining. The world *isn't*, but they are because they believe it so strongly.

As a consequence and often out of sheer frustration or cynicism or anger, people aren't going to readily support you and your ideas if those ideas are different. They'd rather explain to you why life, being difficult, isn't going to let you get what you want. The bottom line in life is, getting what you want (or closer to it) makes you happy and *not* getting what you want (or farther from it) makes you unhappy. Everyone will at least agree with that!

With regard to other people's opinions, ideas, lectures, reactions, feedback, suggestions, counsel, warnings, advice, preaching, conversations, life stories, and so on, one essential rule for getting to Genius thinking and productivity is simple: **don't pay attention to what other people think, otherwise you can't fully be yourself and that's where the Genius is for you—in *you*, not in them.** How can you hear yourself if you're paying attention to them?

It's important to know why that is so. You are unique in all the universe. The person that is attempting to give you advice has had a unique life of their own and is a fundamentally *different* person than you are. Your background is *different*, your education is *different*, the influential people in your life were *different*, your thinking and most intimate beliefs about life are *different*, your expectations and aspirations are *different*, your key formative experiences in life are *different*; in short, your life has already been significantly *different* from theirs and your self-image, identity and what you happen to believe about yourself are also profoundly *different*.

No one else has a cookie-cutter—*commoditized*—solution they can offer you that will work for you. If they did, then everyone would be successful. Do you see everyone being successful? Of course not.

There is no *commoditization* (one-size fits all) of human beings, despite how much we want this to be possible. Wouldn't life be insanely boring if it were?! We'd all be doing exactly the same things and thinking in exactly the same ways, managing exactly the same projects while aspiring to exactly the same results and the same identity.

You can't listen to other people because they don't know what they're talking about when it comes to *you* and also, when you listen to them you are ignoring the voice of the one person that *can* counsel you usefully to success, the one person that *does* have the solutions for you, that *can* lead you to success. That person is *you*.

Geniuses listen intently to *their own voice*, not to the voices of other people no matter how "successful" they may be. They do, however, engage in interactions with other people, but not for the reasons that you may think. We'll get to that later, in our conversation about non-linearity.

The person who is going to educate you about your thinking is *you*.

It is estimated that the "self-help" industry in the United States generates over $10 billion a year in revenue, much of it in books, seminars and videos. People hope and believe that a bigger and better life is possible for them—defined by *getting what they want*—if they only knew how to do it. They tend to think someone *else* can tell them how, but they never find the right person with the right solutions for them. That is mostly impossible.

The problem with self-help is that it is actually *other*-help, not *self*-help. The comedian George Carlin once said this, years ago, in one of his stand-up routines: "Why do they call it *self*-help if its *someone else* doing it!?"

With "self-help," the solutions don't really come from *yourself* at all, they come from *other people* telling you about *their* experiences, talking about the solutions that worked for *them*, addressing what *they* think you should do, and giving you *their* prescriptions for situations and issues they don't really know about at all because they are *your* issues... as if human beings were just plug-and-play commodities that produce the same behaviors under similar circumstances. As if human beings were just cogs in an industrial assembly-line . . . or items on a Gant chart. How is that *self-help*?

In an on-line article titled "**Disobedient Children Make More Money as Adults**," yahoo.com reports on research carried out by the University of Luxembourg, the University of Illinois at Urbana-Champaign, and the Free University of Berlin, that was published in the journal "Development Psychology." It suggests that "those who defied authority as kids tended to have higher incomes as grownups."

In discovering their uniqueness, children have to push against the institutions and individuals who are trying to turn them into commodities, like the impossible concept of a "normal child" and "good" boys and girls. "Normal" doesn't exist in any realm, we just like to pretend that it does. The concept of being normal is used as a weapon against people who attempt to be themselves and think and act differently. Geniuses often act like rebels but the point isn't the rebellion, it's about the liberty of being who they really want to be.

You are unique in that you have a universe of an identity that defines who you are and that doesn't have much to do with what other people have experienced and happen to recommend. That also happens to be true of every project— each has its own agreements, understandings, experiences, ideas and so on, because it is composed of people. In many ways, every project is an entity in its own right.

Businesses dedicate billions to producing carefully defined outcomes in carefully defined periods of time. However, the failure rate is still consistently, extremely high.

The consulting group calleam.com presents a McKinsey & Company study—you can find plenty of these from many sources on the web, incidentally—that gives an idea of the magnitude of what is involved:

A study of 5,400 large scale IT projects (projects with initial budgets greater than $15M) finds that the well-known problems with IT Project Management are persisting. Among the key findings quoted from the report:

1.   17 percent of large IT projects go so badly that they can threaten the very existence of the company;

2.   On average, large IT projects run 45 percent *over* budget and 7 percent *over* time, while delivering 56 percent *less* value than predicted.

These disastrous results are only an example; there are plenty of surveys of IT companies and their projects that show even worse results. Mediocrity is the rule in the management of most projects. Don't take our word for it, although if you are reading this book you're probably already aware of it. Look it up! Read some of the research. It's very easy to find. Just don't spend too much time there; it's not uplifting reading. As you'll see when we discuss problem-solving, understanding the problem won't help you solve it.

Usually, the failures attributed to "well-known problems" and these are said to include phenomena like unrealistic expectations; decision-making that doesn't work, lack of expertise; unresolved strategic issues within the organization; faulty training; poor communication; and, in sum, many seemingly unsolvable problems. If you try to figure out solutions for each of these, like the sorcerer's apprentice in the Goethe poem (and the Disney movie, "Fantasia"), you'll not only never catch up, the problem will keep getting worse and worse.

People everywhere are blind to the real causes of the gaping difference between what they want and what they get, and their usual instinct is to *analyze the situation further*, and then to come up with a list of *measures to be taken,* not knowing that it is precisely *that* linear form of thinking—breaking things down into fragments and then lining them up into a sequence—that is the real heart of the problem. It leads to bigger and bigger problems, escalating the losses. Once you've identified a problem, further analysis just makes the problem worse.

Yes, "project management" does involved "breaking things down into fragments and then lining them up in a sequence," but in order to be successful, that's relatively insignificant in determining success. It's a threshold capability. As we explained, you need to have it to get in the door as a project manager, but more of it makes absolutely no difference for producing superior performance. Anyone can think in linear terms about project management. Everyone does!

You can't come up with a useful solution, you can't "think outside of the box" that you find yourself in, when *it is actually your very thinking that is the box: linear thinking.*

The Information Age will consistently, endlessly distract you from you. There is no catching up with it. There is no "information app" or process or software that can hold back the flood. You can follow all sorts of recommendations for getting your e-mail up to date and you will still never catch up. Tomorrow you'll face the same or worse. Linearity has massive momentum that can only really be by *non-linearity.*

Have you noticed how, the farther we get into the Information Age, the more desperately we look for—and are offered—ways of handling all that information? People address information, in their search for solutions, as if the problem was one of volume, which it isn't. That's part of the search for categories as "buckets," as if you could control the exponential spewing of information in the world by using more buckets to put it all in. We are about as successful at this as the sorcerer's apprentice was in mopping up all that water and putting it in buckets.

You will never have enough "buckets," no matter how many you design. Linearity loves coming up with new categories for things. From innovation to productivity, academics and consultants are churning out new definitions and new categories, and new "drawers" and files to put them in. Linear thinking cannot solve information problems, it can only generate more of them. That is its nature. That is what it is designed for. If you have alternatives, then they aren't problems any longer, but those alternatives have to be entirely different ways of thinking.

Information cannot solve information problems.

In organizations, an overload of strictly controlled information generates **hierarchies**, and the hierarchies, like the information, become more and more pronounced as the organization grows. Titles proliferate, as do new job descriptions and organization charts and they change all the time.

"Flat" organizations don't work, because the attempt is based on designing characteristics that are peripheral to human thinking and end up making little or no difference. What can make them flatter is greater transparency, particularly in decision-making, not an organization chart.

More and more information generates more and more rules, policies and politics about *who* makes *which* decisions, using *what* information. You'd think the information age would make this easier. Isn't this really about so-called "knowledge management?" Well, of course it isn't.

Today in most organizations we have many more managers than are really needed. They mystify their jobs by not sharing their decisions or their decision-making criteria (see the article titled "**The End of Management**," by J. Santiago Pedrosa). The more information an organization has to deal with, the worse this phenomenon gets. Managers need to make themselves seem useful, even indispensable, and so they obfuscate what they're really doing. They may even be worried that their employees may find out just how much they *don't* know or how little they are really accomplishing. (Geniuses never worry about that.)

Hierarchies are produced when decision-making and access to key information are strictly controlled. If these aren't openly shared and discussed, the organization moves to ever more complex hierarchies. Organizations think they can design flat organizations, motivated either by an altruistic ideal or the mistaken idea that this will make work easier. They don't understand how and why hierarchies are created.

It's also an example about how information usually has, in general, two stages of effects: an immediate effect (reaction), and a longer-term effect (changing the institutions and media in which it operates). Take a look at our political communication and institutions and you can readily see what we mean. The institutions are changing under their feet and they still persistently focus on reacting to trivia.

With information technology, our jobs went from 40 hours a week to 24/7. Just thirty or so years ago, a client couldn't reach you "after hours." They had to leave a message and you would get back to them the next day. Today, that client is in your pocket even when you take a break to go to the restroom. Isn't this the technology that was supposed to make our jobs and lives easier? Even "multi-tasking," which has been proven to be a myth, based on what the brain is actually doing during that activity, has acquired status and dedication among people who don't realize they are sinking deeper into the quicksand. They react to trivia while the real game is changing the rules.

Technology trains us to *notice* and to *react* but not to *know*. The capacity for intimacy and the possibilities for knowledge diminish, the more information we pay attention to. Waking consciousness—our primary form of awareness—doesn't have the bandwidth to handle both information and knowledge.

It is a surprising effect of the Information Age that it moves us *away* from knowledge *towards* information and reaction. Innovation, problem solving, and unprecedented successful results are about *knowing*, not about being informed. You really have to be deliberate if you want to *know*.

There are many start-ups with novel software for managing information, with new ways to search for a document on your computer for example, new ways to present the information, new ways to send it and new ways to get it into the cloud. This proliferation of information control "solutions" will never end because people will always hope that one of them will actually solve things for them. Still, information technology will always generate more information than people can reasonably ever handle with a linear approach.

In this book, we will show how Genius project managers handle this. They get exceptional results and are known for it. You can do this too, because Geniuses don't have a genetic quality that others don't have. They didn't come into the world neurologically "gifted;" their intense desire and their reactions to their life experiences *made them* (brain plasticity—repeated experiences that end up changing the brain) neurologically gifted. They understand the language of Genius, which has been deprecated, dismissed and ignored deliberately for over a thousand years. You aren't aware of it, but dismissing and deprecating your own Genius has already been a big part of your "education."

Your brain already uses the language of Genius. It uses *two* languages but you only learn to use *one*. Only Geniuses use them both *deliberately*. We all learn the languages we are taught in school, the languages of words and numbers.

Western culture can be said to be an advanced culture that was built based on illusions. People are adamant about speaking only one language while living in a body with a brain that speaks *two*.

The language we use and know well, we call *linearity* and it consists mainly of numbers, code and words. Linearity is what we usually mean by "language." Linear languages are certainly useful, but are only a *part* of what's happening in the real world. That's why most projects are not finished on time, are not finished on budget, and do not reflect excellence. **The part of reality they are addressing is too limited.**

Two Languages Spoken by Two Minds

Did you ever notice how innovations and solutions to problems and great ideas always seem out of reach? ...like they're hiding from us? Here we are, intelligent and experienced adults, and we can't easily innovate or solve problems—two consist demands in most business situations—which are sold with the persistent, holy myth of "hard work."

Why is that? Shouldn't all this be really *easy*? Why is innovation easy for Geniuses and hard for everyone else? Do they have some exceptional capacity we're never told about? ...because the truth is, any Genius we learn about is never explained to us in such a way that we could say, "Oh! I get it! No wonder!" No, there is always something "magical" and exceptional about them that is never explained. There are no Geniuses of hard work.

Geniuses are made to seem like extra-terrestrial beings who came to earth to do their Genius thing. Have you noticed this? Why is that?

The strange thing is, once we explain it fully you'll see that Genius is within anyone's reach. **It's just that no one understand it.** Why does no one understand it? You'd think that in the 21st century this would all be clear by now.

It will be clear; we're going to explain it to you. Think of it this way. Say you go to Helsinki, Finland, and you sit in on a meeting. You don't speak Finnish at all. At the end, you are asked what you understood, as they explained—in Finnish—the secrets of the universe, which you are not familiar with.

You definitely would not understand *anything*, and you would know as much about the secrets of the universe as when you first when into the meeting, which would be absolutely nothing. It's exactly the same situation.

When we say Geniuses speak a different language, that's exactly what we mean—*a completely different language.* We can't emphasize enough how important it is to know this, even just to use this book. In **Part 2, Non-Linearity,** we go into that second language, the "Finnish" that Geniuses use, but you will be tempted to expect to use it like the linear language that you already know. We will remind you, that won't work.

The two languages we are referring to are used by what we call *waking consciousness* and the *non-conscious mind*. Those are the two terms we prefer for these, although there are many other terms that are often used. The non-conscious is often called the *sub*-conscious or the *un*-conscious, for example. Waking consciousness is usually simply referred to as consciousness.

Waking consciousness seems to be, when we are in it, a continuous mental state of alertness, of taking in what's happening and being able to readily act and think. It actually isn't continuous at all, but that's only because it's doing its inevitable deception (more on that later). The truth is that during any given time period, we are not continuously in a state of mental alertness at all.

We actually move to many different mental states in any given time period. We may remember something and think about it for a second or two; it may surface a feeling we like (or don't); we may drift off for a few seconds or micro-seconds into some kind of daydreaming state; we may be mentally analyzing something so intently that we aren't fully aware of what's happening around us until we are startled or in some way "brought back" to the physical reality we find ourselves in; we think about lunch because our stomach is grumbling, and so on. All of this is a perfectly normal part of being human and experiencing waking consciousness. We only think that waking consciousness is perfectly continuous and uninterrupted, but it isn't.

The *non*-conscious mind is where all significant innovations and solutions come from. They "come to mind;" that is, they *come to* waking consciousness but they are not *produced by it*.

Waking consciousness only has two main functions: *focus* **(or "attention"), which allows us to decide what we want; the other, a necessary consequence of its limited bandwidth, is** *deception,* which leads us to think that we are viewing all of reality when we're only exposed to an infinitesimally tiny fraction of it.

Everything else—which is most everything—is handled by the non-conscious mind. Did you determine how to filter your entire body's blood supply in the last 5 minutes, which is when that took place? No. Your non-conscious handled it. How did you parse out your gastric juices, or your hormones, or your blood pressure...?

We think of an "intelligent" entity as one that can gather information, assess it, determine what to do with it, and make useful decisions—based on higher outcomes—that optimize the achievement of those outcomes, given the resources and time available. Your non-conscious mind is doing this in your body billions and billions of times every instant, with so many inputs and decisions that you're waking consciousness could never even *conceive* of them.

Think of it like downhill skiing. Can a downhill skier tell you what and how they actually do what they do? No they can't. As with most Geniuses, if you ask them how to do what they do, they will invariably tell you, "Well, you have to work really hard!" That is the default answer you will be given by someone who doesn't really know at all how they make things happen, and most people don't. It doesn't matter if they can't explain *how*; their achievements don't depend on that at all.

A downhill skier relies on his/her physical body's knowledge and the emotional and physical sensations he/she experiences in the moment. Is there time, while traveling on skis at over 60 miles per hour, to analyze situations? Of course not. The skier is operating by *instinct*, which is *non-conscious* and is feeling-based. It seems like it's his body making the instant decision, micro-second by micro-second. It is. It's the non-conscious mind with its own language, the language of feeling.

Yes, if you work really, really hard, over and over, you may learn some of those movements. Then again, you may also get yourself killed. Practice is useful only if it's used in the right context. What we call "practice" is really just one of the ways in which waking consciousness makes decisions about what it wants, and communicates them to the non-conscious in its language—through *feeling*. Practice is the process of waking consciousness identifying what it wants and what it *doesn't* want—its *only* job.

In 1962 Thomas S. Kuhn wrote a brilliant book on the history of science titled "**The Structure of Scientific Revolutions**," where he described scientific progress in terms of new "paradigms"—a paradigm is a mental framework with its own, defined ways of thinking. A new paradigm accompanies any profoundly revolutionary idea. If you were a university student studying science during the 1970's, Kuhn's book was required reading even if you weren't in a science program.

Kuhn was addressing new discoveries in physics. He understood the processes that help activate the creation of these ideas, *and* he was clear about where they come from:

> "Paradigms are not corrigible by normal science at all."

Kuhn is referring to the fact that no matter how much data we discover that indicates that our world view/paradigm is *mistaken*, and we need the discovery of a *new* paradigm to correct our understanding of that data, "normal science"—which we can take to mean the normal, waking consciousness thinking about science—cannot produce it. Normal science...

> ...ultimately leads only to the recognition of anomalies and to crises. And these are terminated, not by deliberation and interpretation, but by a relatively sudden and unstructured event... Scientists then speak of the '**scales falling from the eyes**' or of the '**lightning flash**' that 'inundates a previously obscure puzzle, **enabling is components to be seen in a new way that for the first time permits its solution.** On the other hand, the relevant illumination comes in sleep. [Kuhn here cites Jacques Hadamard on "subconscious intuition."] No ordinary sense of the term 'interpretation' fits these **flashes of intuition** through which a new paradigm is born. (Kuhn, p. 123). [Boldface ours.]

In other words, while waking consciousness ("normal science") can recognize and identify the anomalies and crises, it cannot resolve them by generating a new idea. That must come from somewhere *else*.

Kuhn's ideas themselves created a new paradigm in how we understand how science and its discoveries develop. They had long been considered a logical, rational progression of linear, incremental, conscious "interpretations." That is not at all true. Scientific progress is a mixture of, first, consciously discovering anomalies, and second, having solutions and new paradigms "come to mind." **That's consciousness identifying what it wants (the solution to this dilemma), and the non-conscious providing the "flash" (it "comes to mind.")**

It takes a different mental state that is *not* based on analysis or interpretation that invites the *non*-conscious mind in, in order for the solutions to "come to mind."

In Marc Lewis' book, **"The Biology of Desire, Why Addiction is Not a Disease"** (2015) we learn how our diagnoses of addiction as a disease are mistaken, despite the fact that there is even legislation supported by medical doctors advocating for that very diagnosis. The disease perspective robs people of agency over their own lives.

In general, people who call these experiences "disorders" are people who don't experience them themselves, and so don't consider them "normal" behavior. Lewis writes, "The brain evolved to pursue goals by focusing attention and motivation on likely sources of pleasure or relief, especially those right in front of our noses." (Lewis).

These disorders of attention, ADHD, OCD, addiction and depression among them, are simply the brain doing the job it was designed for and possibly, doing it too insistently in self-reinforcing loops.

What is the use of focus? Focus enables Geniuses to respond intelligently to the most important question of their lives, the question that drives their Genius forward: **"What do I want?"**

Nothing can be more important, because the answer to that question which granted, may change often, provides content for a Genius' identity. Ultimately, Genius is about who you think you are, and nobody else needs to know but you.

The most important product of consciousness is that with its ability to *focus*, that is, to select a central point and place its attention on it, not on the surrounding context, we can respond to the all-important question, "What do I want?" The non-conscious mind cannot focus in that way and so *the non-conscious mind does not initiate desire*. The answers to the question mutates over time in important and useful ways. Ultimately, **being a Genius is a powerful feeling about your own identity.**

Focus is often called *attention*. In the Information Age, people prefer the term "attention" but we feel that it is broader than the term "focus," and the whole point of both is to zero in narrowly on something, whether material or intangible, to isolate it from what is in contrast to it. Waking consciousness can focus on either what is material or on what is intangible: look at the book you have in your hands; imagine it floating in the room. Its powers of focus are exceptional which is good, because waking consciousness doesn't really do much else.

The awareness we call waking consciousness looks at reality through a keyhole. We think we are seeing the whole picture, but we really are only getting a keyhole view. In fact, researchers have estimated for some time that waking consciousness can only absorb at most, about 40 bits of information per second. That isn't much.

Non-conscious thinking, however, based on the number of individual neurons involved, has the capacity to take in up to about 40 *million* bits per second. Tors Nørretranders, in his **"The User Illusion, Cutting Consciousness Down to Size,"** spends quite a bit of time on this topic, as it is central to his research and thesis.

Although there are different ways of defining and measuring these "bits" and what they mean in the human brain, what is important isn't so much the absolute numbers as the mammoth difference in proportions between the oceans of data absorbed by the non-conscious in contrast with the narrow trickle of information captured by waking consciousness. However you choose to define it, we have known about this contrast in their proportions for decades.

Add to this all of the intelligent entities in the human body. If we define "intelligence" as the capacity to make appropriate and beneficial decisions when faced with a variety of alternatives, then there are many organs and other parts of the human body that are intelligent in their own right.

Are you now aware of the functioning of the lymphatic system in your body, or digestion, or the circulatory system? Vital and complex, intelligent decisions are being made inside your body all the time. There are many forms of non-conscious physical and mental awareness. They are going on without the participation of waking consciousness. Waking consciousness cannot handle that volume of data, much less make decisions about it.

In fact, these days brain neurologists prefer to call the brain the *embodied* brain, because our concept of a separation of the body from the brain, as if it were an unrelated body fragment, is nonsensical. The body participates actively and continuously in brain function.

The model we have of body and brain function is still fundamentally an Industrial Age model, but then so are our models for education and learning and for innovation and problem-solving. Until we can see linearity in proper perspective instead of thinking that it composes all of reality, we'll continue to be entities in a body with a brain that speaks at least two languages while we use only one.

Project management has historically been designed, understood and measured under rigid terms of linearity. The success of projects is measured entirely as a succession of fragments that were designed in advance. Success in this sense means that your project proceeded "according to plan;" it met all the pre-designed expectations, especially timeframes and costs.

Unfortunately, this actually doesn't happen very often! When you examine the success/failure rates of most projects, technological or otherwise, "failure" is actually the norm. That's the legacy of linearity. It sees the project through the "keyhole" of waking consciousness, relying only on what is visible and on what can be measured.

Reality is more complex and much bigger than that, but linearity doesn't allow for it. That is why certifications in project management, forms of measurement, software and all manner of control still don't do the job. Still, linear thinking will continue devising new ways to exert itself and will still fail most of the time.

What is Linearity, Exactly?

Linearity is in everything we produce. We are very thoughtful about linear language and consider it a virtue for things to be linear. We consider non-linearity, whatever it may be, as something unwanted, confusing, chaotic, and even execrable.

Linearity means things are lined up, one after the other like cars in a train, like machinery in an assembly line. To line things up, we first have to have **fragments** to line up, like the cars or the machinery. Linearity takes things apart, then puts them back together in order, but not just in any order. So that they make sense and to create value, things have to be lined up in a particular **sequence**.

A sequence is a particularly ordered linear phenomenon. That sequence adapts the parts of the product to the machinery, or the project idea to the budget that is available. We take sequences and linearity so for granted that we aren't really aware of how they make up much of our external reality. They especially make up the language parts of our reality.

Think of the word "**sequence**." We could line up the letters that make up this word in many ways. "**Qncseuee**" is one way, for example. It contains exactly the same letters of the alphabet, but obviously it makes no sense at all, so it has no value (except in making the point we're making about meaning). We already have an agreement on the word sequence and what it means. That agreement is useful because it means the same for everyone. What we call *literacy* handled that. Literacy is one of the infinite forms of linearity. It is our greatest concern for little children to master.

When we went to school as children, we first learned that things have to line up (even the children!). When it comes to any language, things especially have to line up *exactly*. In school, we called the early part of our learning "spelling." There are competitions to see who best masters spelling. There are no competitions to see who masters *non*-linearity because to begin with, people don't even know what it is.

As we grew older and went through more schooling, we learned many more forms of order and sequence, depending on the areas of study and career we choose. All academic disciplines are based on this. You are obligated to choose a career for your "higher education." That career already has built-in definitions, categories and strict linearity's of all kinds. There is a website for jobs and careers called "ladders" for those reasons. Your career is seen as a vertical assembly line. First one rung, then the next.

As a consequence, some people think that linearity has something to do with knowledge, understandably, but it doesn't. Some people think that you can't think without language, when language is actually the very least of it. That's a testament to how much we value linearity.

Languages are linear because they are composed of fragments—letters or ideographs or drawings—and these are placed in a meaningful sequence. Computer code is always the sequencing of fragments:
settextstyle(TRIPLEX_FONT,HORIZ_DIR is a sequence.

Any use of numbers that has meaning, forms a sequence, such as **21 + 2 = 23**. Anything that is accounting, such as spreadsheets and profit-and-loss statements, for example, are sequences. All sequences adhere to very demanding, detailed protocols. Protocols are rules for linearity. In spelling we have protocols like the one for exceptions (For example, "i" before "e" except after "c," or when sounded as "a," as in "neighbor" or "weigh.")

The protocols for sequences in any language are always very many, because languages create many versions of themselves and there are endless exceptions. No matter what topic you pick in technology, it will of course be defined with a protocol for its sequencing of data into information. People take these rules very seriously. Currently, for example, there is a debate about the "correctness" of leaving two spaces after a period in a text, versus leaving just one.

Context is why information is always incomplete. The context can never be fully expressed with the language and the message. There's always something missing that linearity cannot address, although it's not for lack of trying. Context is a form of hidden content that gets assumed by sender and receiver, which is often the source of many misunderstandings because the parts that aren't articulated are expected to be understood or assumed equally by both sender and receiver. Any context is part of an infinite Venn diagram.

Contexts can relate, almost endlessly, to different kinds of information. English geography is part of the context for World War II (1939 – 1945), but so is the Treaty of Versailles (1919). You can see that context depends on perspective, which is the view you have from wherever you happen to be standing, that is, whatever you happen to be focusing on. That's why it's so easy for people to disagree on things!

Context is a very individual thing. Perspective and context for one person, or for one situation, aren't necessarily the same for another person or situation at all. We tend to communicate as if they were, which is another way of saying that people make assumptions about what other people know or don't know, and they act on them. They sometimes become infuriated when the other person doesn't have the same perspective that they do. Not having the right context absolutely decimates the information that is piled on it.

You can't write enough detail to answer all the possible answers to questions on a given topic, for example. The assembly line of linear thinking always has an ending; it isn't infinite; something is always missing. You can't have enough information to handle the need for information because that would require all the information in the universe.

Whomever you approach to have them give you a summary of a project that is underway, is going to give you enough context to suit *their* assessment of what you need to know and that will never be all of it, only a subset of information that seems appropriate to the moment and the circumstances and the sender and receiver, because you don't have all the time in the world to listen to the infinite number of linear explanations and inventories of information that are involved. It's a question of "best-guess" scenarios.

Again, this is how **information itself is never enough**. Thinking that information *is* enough when it really isn't, is one of the major ways in which projects fail. Remember, we're talking about information, not knowledge. When people think that information can be enough, that gets them into big trouble; they don't understand the difference. The *knowledge* of what is really going on is often staring them in the face all the while. It's that uncomfortable feeling in their gut, for example, that they've been trying to ignore.

Information is always a best-guess of what is required for a given situation; there has to be a point where we have to "pull the plug" on delivering more information. That's why the Information Age is the age in which we learned that **there is never enough information**—not in communicating through linearity, anyway. The problem that people have with the Information Age is that while they are abundantly *informed*, they don't really *know*.

Protocols help avoid having to explain too much context. They are a form of "short-hand" (another language that used to exist before electronic devices replaced them). Still, as is always the fate of linearity, most of the context will go unexplained. This is true for all projects. Think of all the context that a new team member will never learn, or will only learn small pieces of, for example...

- The background experiences that drive the political and organizational motivations of other team members;

- The organization's own history and key, cultural myths;

- The unspoken expectations about boundaries and how to be treated;

- Proper project team "etiquette" in the organization's culture;

- The dimensions of the infamous "box" that no one can really "think outside" of, as much as they try...

Any place that numbers are part of your life—your bank statement, the restaurant's dinner receipt, the list of phone numbers on your cell phone—are all based on sequences. The numbers have meaning because they are part of a well-known sequence and its related protocols.

That sequence is part of a larger context that no longer has to be explained because you've learned it and used it so often. For example, when you finish your meal in a restaurant, the waiter hands you a small slip of paper with numbers on it. You understand what it means and exactly what the alternatives are for responding appropriately.

In natural languages we use letters to create **words**, which we then use to create **phrases** or **sentences**, which then create **paragraphs**, which can in turn create **chapters, e-mail messages** or other types of documents like proposals, performance reviews, job descriptions, job applications, petitions, twitter.com messages, grocery lists and so on. They will all have more **assumed, unstated context** than **explicitly stated content**.

There is a historical era that accelerated literacy across Europe, with the proliferation of many different kinds of media. There were actually many forms of "social media," except that term wasn't in use at the time. That era was the French Revolution (1789 – 1799), which included a massive proliferation of **newsletters, newspapers, magazines, leaflets, books, proposals, legislation, notes, amendments, agreements, posters and handbills**, among many others. Today, we might think they are too primitive to be considered social media because they aren't electronic, but they served the same functions.

Media of all kinds are simply massive, public ways to organize languages, including visual languages like photographs, pictures, video and video clips, all into a more manageable form. Media are just massive categories for information in different kinds of sequences. All media are based on fragments ordered in sequences and then collected, copied, distributed and presented in *larger* categories of sequences like films, blogs, photo books, tumblr.com pages, project plans, lists of stakeholders and many others.

Some people consider the increasingly complex volumes of information, ordered into larger and larger categories with more sophisticated relationships and nomenclature, as forms of knowledge. They call this process "Knowledge Management," but they're not managing knowledge at all.

These processes all use fragments (knowledge does not) and are in reality, just more sophisticated, more capacious forms of information control. "Knowledge Management" as a particular discipline in the business world, is and will always be *information control.*

We like to think we can keep knowledge under control but we don't want to be "controlling," so we avoid that term. "Knowledge" sounds more sophisticated and complex than "information;" "management" sounds more sophisticated and complex than "control." So what is really "information control" is called "knowledge management," which comes with its own sequences and protocols. It's easy for linearity to create new definitions and to manipulate meaning. Ask any politician!

These categories are a way we attempt to makes sense of all the fragments that information is incessantly throwing our way. In project management, we have categories of projects and we have timelines with stages or phases. Categories help us keep track of the flood of information we are receiving, so we begin to think we can handle that flood thanks to the categories, even though we really can't.

So-called "value chains," with fragments all lined up in the perceived sequence, are another of many examples of linear explanations of realities which are ultimately too complex to be understood as linear. They are part of the scientific mythology that says that strict, one-to-one cause and effect relationships can explain multi-dimensional phenomena.

Analysis and naming things don't change the reality we are dealing with, but they do add to our nomenclature and give us a sense that "things are under control." Geniuses, however, are not easily deceived by the mere appearance of things. Non-linearity—feeling—gives them a reliable "deception-detector" (sometimes called a "bullshit detector;" see Neil Postman's excellent book, **"Teaching as a Subversive Activity**," 1971).

Since linearity can't represent *all* the infinite details of context, something is always missing; since something is always missing, there is always (unintended) deception. That's also why it's so easy to create conspiracy theories! Conspiracy theories, partially devoid of actual facts, always depend on the listener or reader to fill in the blanks.

The real problem we are usually facing but don't see, is the problem of *meaning*. If we look at all communication as based on attempting to discover and communicate meaning, we can see that **the real issue in the Information Age is the *lack* of information, not an over-abundance of information**.

That is a surprise to most people. We want *meaning*. There is no point to information without meaning. Take this example: **"8&9ddle 1 a C**." That's data and it *is* in a sequence. However, it doesn't seem to correspond to any category or protocol that we know or use. What does it mean? Well, it doesn't mean anything at all, because we just made it up. It doesn't qualify as information although it does seem to include data that we use in other categories that have meaning.

All information comes from data. Data consists of (practically) irreducible, small items that don't make much sense alone. Numbers are data; letters are data. The use of any language, whether it uses words, numbers or code, is ultimately for the purpose of creating, expressing, storing, editing and communicating *meaning*. Without meaning, there is no point.

Information is composed of data, like **bits**, which in technology are meant to represent the smallest units of binary mathematical languages used for code. 01000001 is the capital letter "A" in binary code. If you think of the sequence that gives data meaning, then you can see how **information is always *data, in formation*.** If you don't have the right sequence you can't make sense because the data won't be **in** the proper **formation.**

Information is always just data, in formation. **It is not *knowledge* which, based as it is on feeling, and which isn't *fragmented* and *sequential* but rather *whole* and *instantaneous*.**

Meaning always goes back to the context that the data came from in the first place, and context is always broad and complex. When you send an e-mail message to someone, the context is different—as with all messages—depending on whom you are sending it to, what you want to say, when you are sending it and many other variables.

There is so much context you couldn't possibly explain it all but fortunately you don't have to. That's much of the beauty of the categories of information. If it's an e-mail message to my boss, it's going to have a different context than my comment on a 360° performance review of him or her.

Over the years, youtube.com has published newer and newer versions of a video that went viral very quickly when it first appeared in 2006. It's titled "**Did You Know?**"

Created by Karl Fisch and Scott McLeod, it documents (with a great Fatboy Slim song as background) what it calls the *exponential* growth of everything digital. For example, "did you know...?" says that "we live in exponential times," and that... ("**Did You Know? Shift Happens, 2014 Remix**"):

- There are 5.9 billion searches on Google every day;

- Every day, the total number of text messages sent and received is double the total population of the planet;

- It took radio 38 years to reach a market audience of 50 million; it took Angry Birds Space 35 *days*;

- It is estimated that 4 Exabyte's (4 x 10^{19} –that's *19* zeros) of unique information will be generated just this year;

- The amount of new, technical information doubles every 2 years;

- 90 % of the world's existing data has been generated in the past 2 years.

There is however, one statistic that we laugh at every time we see it: "Predictions are that by 2049, a computer will exceed the computational capabilities of the entire human species."

We laugh, because computation is a minor human capability and not one that concerns us. That's precisely why we have *computers*—for *computation*. There is no talk of consciousness in these statistics, of course; waking consciousness is assumed. There is certainly no talk about the one, major characteristic that gives us life: *desire*. **Technology informs us on an infinite number of topics but it knows absolutely nothing about desire.**

Your Consciousness Does NOT Do What You Think!

It's important to understand the limitations of waking consciousness, because that will impress upon you more and more the importance of learning to deliberately use the *non*-conscious mind. It's been waiting for you.

Waking consciousness—the awareness you have right now as you read this—has two primary functions and one of these is deceiving us into thinking that it can see and understand all of reality. That is not the case. The analogy we use is that waking consciousness is like looking through a keyhole into another room and thinking that you can see the whole room.

The *non*-conscious mind, however, is like throwing open the door to that room—it's just that we aren't there consciously to see what's in there directly! We have to create the mental conditions for the non-conscious mind to reveal to us through its own language, what it is that's there.

As Julian Jaynes, author of a book on consciousness that we will reference shortly, described it, waking consciousness is like using a flashlight to see in a dark room. You can't see what isn't lit by the flashlight, which is most of what's there, but the fact that you can't see it (you can't be conscious of it) doesn't mean it's not there.

The non-conscious mind can and does capture millions more bits of data per second than our waking awareness, but our waking awareness needs to make itself known, considered, taken into account somehow, because it does have a very fundamental role and it is very good at it. In fact, it really has only one role; what we're calling the second role is just for control and credibility in what it offers and is a consequence of miniscule bandwidth. Waking consciousness answers the single most important question for our projects—and indeed, for our lives: ***what do you want?*** <u>Nothing is more important than that</u>. It is who you are.

There are other functions that we like to believe are carried out by waking consciousness, but we know through experimentation that they are not.

The late Julian Jaynes of Princeton University wrote a brilliant chapter on the limits of human consciousness, in his seminal book (often called one of the most significant works in science in the 20th century), "**The Origin of Consciousness in the Breakdown of the Bicameral Mind**" (1976).

As Jaynes memorably puts it, "Consciousness is a much smaller part of our mental life than we are conscious of, because we cannot be conscious of what we are not conscious of." He demonstrates, example by example, one by one, that consciousness is not necessary for creating or understanding concepts; consciousness is not necessary for learning; consciousness is not necessary for thinking; and that consciousness is not necessary for reasoning.

We quote further because it's important to understand, on the one hand, the limitations of waking consciousness and what it does not do, so that on the other hand, we can ultimately better understand what the non-conscious mind does do.

> We have been brought to the conclusion that consciousness [Jaynes' term for waking consciousness] is not what we generally think it is. It is not to be confused with reactivity. It is not involved in hosts of perceptual phenomena. It is not involved in the performance of skills and often hinders

their execution. It does not need to be involved in speaking, writing, listening or reading. . . . It is not necessary for making judgments or in simple thinking. It is not the seat of reason, and indeed some of the most difficult instances of creative reasoning go on without any attending consciousness. And it has no location except an imaginary one! . . .

Here it is only necessary to conclude that consciousness does not make all that much difference to a lot of our activities. (Jaynes, pp. 46-47).

Obviously, if (waking) consciousness is *not* carrying out these functions, then it is the *non*-conscious mind that *is*.

Jaynes' observations are echoed by Tor Nørretranders in his **"The User Illusion, Cutting Consciousness Down to Size"** (p. 153):

The possibility of the lie is the one cost of consciousness. Consciously one can lie, unconsciously one cannot. The lie detector, for example, is proof of this, Karl Steinbuch, of the Technical High School in Karlsruhe, writes in his *Automat and Man*, 1965. 'The possibility of the lie arises precisely because of the low information context of consciousness...'

Deception is part of waking consciousness' nature; there is no malice or bad will of any kind involved. It's just a "now you see it, now you don't" kind of thing. In fact, magicians rely on these illusions to trick you into thinking something has happened that is impossible. The reason for deception is that without it, waking consciousness could not exist! Waking consciousness is tenuous, transitory and tentative. Deception is making us think that on the contrary, it is stable, enduring and confident. We have chosen to believe that illusion to such a degree, that we ignore the part of our mind's that actually does all the heavy lifting.

Experiment 1: A Genius Walks into a Bar...

Here's an experiment that you can carry out to experience the effects and limitations of your waking consciousness' ability to focus, as well as its very limited bandwidth of perception.

In a crowded restaurant or bar where there are a lot of people, listen to the conversations going on around you. There is probably a lot of noise; that's necessary for this test. Pick out two people that are conversing somewhat near you that you can listen to relatively easily without intruding on them.

First, listen to all the noise that you can hear going on inside and outside the restaurant. Listen to the ventilation system, the many conversations, the movement of furniture, the sound of silverware and glasses, sounds from outside traffic, and so on. Move your attention (focus) from one sound to another. This is really easy to do.

Then, listen very intently to the sounds of the conversation of the couple you've chosen to listen to. Listen to the pronunciation and accents of the speakers; try to understand what is being said and what the context might be and in general, immerse yourself in their conversation as much as you can. Then at some point after a few minutes, stop listening to them exclusively and go back to listening to the entire room.

You'll discover that if you listened intently enough to the conversation you chose to focus on, the instant you took your attention off of it and returned to the rest of the room, you'll be briefly aware—very briefly!—that rest of the room had become completely silent. You actually *could not hear* the rest of the room while you were focused on the conversation—*but that perception will only last an instant.*

That's because of the bandwidth—perceptive capacity—limitations of waking awareness. It can't listen to both *one* conversation intently *and* the rest of the restaurant. When you go back to the entire room, that's when for an instant you'll become aware of that "silence" and then quickly, all the other sounds will come roaring back, but in the roar you'll then lose most of the conversation between the two people you were listening to. It takes your conscious mind a fraction of a second to shift its attention.

Visually, we compare this to looking at a room through a keyhole. Waking consciousness isn't going to make it clear to you that you are only seeing through a small hole; it's going to have you believe that you are seeing the entire reality of that room. It has to. If it showed you the full reality, which the non-conscious mind can and does capture, then there would *be* no waking conscious mind at all. Without focus, there is no waking consciousness.

Someone may ask you, "Could you hear the sounds in the rest of the restaurant while you were listening to that particular conversation?" Your response would probably be, "yes," but only because you know that if you moved your attention (or point of focus) from the conversation to the restaurant a large, *you would be able to hear,* even though while you were focused on the conversation, *you could not.*

It seems astounding to us that still today, conversations and recommendations about problem-solving or innovation ignore the single most fundamental, completely proven fact about human mental life and that attempt, regardless of the science and the facts, to have you believe that waking consciousness can innovate or solve problems!

Waking consciousness' deceptions are all based on having us believe that it is doing much more than it is capable of doing. Another, briefer example: your eyes each have a blind spot created by the anatomy of the optic nerve in the eye. Yet in our daily life, we have absolutely no awareness of the blind spot at all. As with many phenomenon, waking consciousness is ensuring that our perception is that our vision is completely uninterrupted and whole. You can experience that blind spot by looking at the two following letters and then moving your attention to only one of them as you move closer to them:

A   B

As your face moves closer and closer to the page, at one point the letter that you are not looking at directly will "disappear." That is the eye's blind spot, which you are never aware of.

The limitations of waking consciousness are a magician's greatest resource; for example, remember being told that "the hand is quicker than the eye" as the magician produces an object that you thought wasn't there?

Focus is a wonderful capacity. Almost all of the so-called "mental disorders" of waking consciousness have to do with focus, including phenomena like Attention Deficit Hyperactive Disorder, Obsessive-Compulsive Disorder, Addiction, and Depression.

We believe that none of these are really disorders at all and research in brain neurology is getting closer and closer to addressing that conclusion. We predict that future neurological research is at some point going to declare that many of these "attention" disorders aren't really disorders at all, just preferences that our minds have for how to work in a variety of situations where they aren't appropriate or useful. With repeated experiences, those preferences can become practically "hard-wired" due to brain plasticity. These are similar to the conclusions affirmed in Marc Lewis' book (**"The Biology of Desire, Why Addiction Is Not a Disease."**)

Some of the History behind Linear Thinking

Linearity is at the heart of the **Industrial Age**, which is an era in human history in which we went from primarily agrarian societies to those based on manufacturing. Manufacturing creates products using assembly lines, which are linearity in physical, material form, composed of a sequence of fragments. Assembly lines were the parents of project management, which is also composed of fragments in a sequence. Its focus is creating commodities, that is, duplicates, sameness, eliminating variations and differences.

Linearity is at the heart of the **Information Age**, which is a subset of the **Industrial Age**, *not* a radically different era, because it is based on the same type of thinking, the same ways of making use of consciousness and the same values. The "industry" is now in digital form, which makes many things easier and faster.

When information serves as a commodity—versus, say, biological information in the body—it also has three important properties, as Luciano Floridi points out in his excellent summary, "**Information, A Very Short Introduction**:"

1. "First, it is non-rivalrous" (one person holding it doesn't mean others cannot);
2. "By default, information tends to be *non-excludable*" or "easily disclosed and shareable."
3. "The cost of its reproduction tends to be negligible." (p. 90).

The Industrial Age used machinery made out of metal and wood to create assembly lines; the Information Age places that assembly line in people's minds as "projects." *Projects are the Information Age's assembly lines.*

The **assembly line** and its progeny in our time, the **project plan**, are both manifestations of linear thinking and in terms of thinking and conception, are virtually the same thing except that assembly lines are ponderous and don't change much, while projects easily change all the time. They both consist of **fragments** arranged in the proper **sequence**, designed to create value. Those fragments are composed of data, in formation.

Commodities, in the sense of being able to create reproducible, duplicate copies of the same thing were, of course, part of the Industrial Age—that's the whole point of industrialization. But in the Information Age, commoditization became unquestioned, which is what accounts in part for the denial of knowledge, which is unique and cannot be commoditized, as you will see, versus information, which is by nature a commodity.

Gutenberg's press was not only the first assembly line, with its movable type, which made it infinitely adaptable for the production of different products. It was also the first **mass medium** and the first **mass social medium**. It also created the first **information commodity** (the Gutenberg Bible).

No one thinks of Johannes Gutenberg (1398 to 1468) as the author of the Information Age because our linear values would have us believe that progress happens only in an orderly, sequential fashion. What comes *later* is supposed to be automatically superior to what happened *before* ("new and improved!"), and no one from the past could have anything to offer that would be actually new and useful to us.

If we looked at the social history of Western civilization we would understand it far differently than we do now, from the perspective of *how we think* and *how conscious awareness develops*. The French Revolution is an example. It was an explosive period of social unrest, to a great degree the product of the expanded use and mastery of literacy, which generated an explosion of media as we have pointed out.

It gave us entirely new concepts that changed our understanding of ourselves and of our society. For example, Marshall McLuhan pointed out in "**The Gutenberg Galaxy**" that the concept of nationalism didn't exist before literacy. There was no territorial, national identity, just collections of kingdoms and dukedoms and principalities and territories and the like. It only happened when groups of people started learning a new identity that nationalism came about. Today, people's identities are manipulated and shifted by media all the time.

How the Inquisition (Unwittingly) Supported Linear Thinking

We have to understand that the language of *feeling*, which is the language of the *non*-conscious mind, has for centuries been depreciated rigorously by philosophers and scientists, even though it's a basic human function that, like breathing, can't be avoided. But it can and has been disparaged as useless or at best, distracting.

A great part of the history that decimated feeling as a topic for research came in historically unexpected ways over the course of centuries. The terrorizing impact of the Catholic Church's Office of the Inquisition, from the 12th through 19th centuries, was directed at the behavior of Catholic heretics who produced their own ideas about science, history and material reality. The Inquisition's stated intention was not primarily to punish heretics, but rather to instill terror in Catholic congregations themselves, whose members might be tempted to follow suit. It was, in a sense and by self-admission, the first terrorist organization.

(Although we don't see it that way, fundamentalist and terrorist organizations—and the two are very similar—are mainly concerned about controlling their population of dedicated followers than they are about people external to the organization.)

The historical reaction to this was immense and long-lasting. It produced the anti-clericalism that fueled research and writing on philosophies and sciences that, through their focus on logic, reason and linearity, would attempt to destroy the Church's belief in the supernatural and in its capricious attempts to control thought and behavior through the emotion of fear.

Everyone knows the case of Galileo, but every scientific thinker during those centuries was subject to potential penalties. The *"Index Librorum Prohibitorum"* was the Church's list of prohibited books; it wasn't abolished until 1966.

Johannes Kepler, Immanuel Kant, Dante Alighieri, René Descartes, Jean-Jacques Rousseau, Galileo Galilei, Johannes Scotus, Nicolaus Copernicus, Maimonides, Baruch Spinoza... as late as 1948, the list contained hundreds authors and of titles. The biographies of many of outstanding thinkers and scientists are riddled with their fear, and the measures they took to avoid confrontation with the Inquisition and from having their books on the **Index**.

The way they dealt with this was to oppose any thinking that might be imbued with superstition, a "lack of rationality," or feeling, as not scientific, as not logical, as not supportable by intelligent intellectuals. This anti-clericalism spawned many movements, such as the *Cult de la Raison* in France, but mainly banished thinking that couldn't be based on materialism and linearity as irrational. It persists in

Western culture today, even when its basic tenets have been clearly disproven.

Thus the powerful, concerted and historical reaction to the Church's efforts to control thought and publications generated an equally—or even more powerful effort—to attack what was understood as irrational thinking or feeling.

Ironically, technology has created new instrumentation that has revolutionized the study of the brain and how it functions. These studies are showing insistently that feeling and emotion aren't secondary, aren't distractions, aren't chemical imbalances, but rather go to the very heart of what human brain function is doing at all times. That is the topic of our next part: the language of the non-conscious mind, which is *feeling*, and how Geniuses use it.

II

Non-Linearity, the Language of Genius

Words Can Give You Information, But Only Feeling Can Give You Knowledge

What is *Non*-Linearity, Exactly?

Non-linearity is *feeling*, a natural human ability and characteristic which is treated as if it didn't exist or as if isn't important. Yet it is not only the most human of all characteristics; it is the very heart of Genius. Feeling is the only *non*-linearity we can know.

Geniuses are able to use an entirely different language than that of linearity. They not only understand it but know how to *call it up*. **Human *feeling* is human *knowledge*.** You won't find it on the servers that hold your (now outdated, static) "knowledge management" files.

The language of Genius doesn't have words because it is vast; words are too limiting. It is the only *non*-linear communication possible in a human body. All other languages we use—code, mathematics, natural languages—are linear, that is, composed of fragments arranged in a sequence. Feelings have no fragments and thus, need no sequence.

Feeling gives you the whole thing and it requires no explanation as to what it is. When you feel something, do you have to wait for the feeling to complete itself, like reading to the end of a sentence? Do you have to piece together the parts? Is there any assembly involved? Do you have to have someone explain to you how you feel? Of course not. Feeling is far too intimate for you *not* to know. **Feeling *is* knowing**.

Non-linearity offers vast amounts of knowledge, in contrast to the tiny, sequential, dribbled fragments of information that linearity offers, which are mostly trivia. We don't think of it that way, because we've learned differently. We think feelings are the trivia—insignificant, accidental or spontaneous chemical reactions that can't be understood. We think of information—which is always incomplete and mostly inconsequential—as somehow vitally important.

Feelings are the manifestation of an identity each person has been building, unknowingly, all his/her life. Your non-conscious has kept track. **Feeling is based on knowledge about who you really are—who you have been aspiring to.** Tell me who you aspire to be, tell me what you want, and I'll tell you who you are. You cannot begin to imagine how much knowledge an adult has generated already in their own life.

First, appreciate feeling and know that it is unique knowledge with valuable uses for you. No one else can ever really *know* it. **Feeling is *embodied information*,** just as we call the brain, the "embodied brain." It is information that no outsider could offer you in a "self-help" book.

Human knowledge is a particular human's embodied information, so complex and vast that it must be held as *feeling* rather than as words.

No one can ever possibly know where someone else *is*. That is the antithesis of linearity, of sameness, of commoditization, of conformity, of expectations... Everyone is fundamentally different from everyone else. No one in the world can ever possibly *know* what someone else has ever experienced—not even close, even if it looks like (linearity) in which someone has had "similar" experiences. No one has ever, in the history of the universe, lived what someone else has lived. All formative experiences are different; so are the impacts of different people, the communications of caregivers, and the experiences both overt and tacit that each person undergoes... No one has ever been where someone else has been or is. This infinite diversity of experience and of knowing is what makes Genius possible.

In this section, we'll explain exactly what non-linearity is and some of the vocabulary we use to describe it. Bear in mind when you read our explanations that we are attempting to describe phenomena that are *non*-linear, in a *linear* medium: this book. So we will make repeated attempts to have you experience the *feeling* level of communication, which is what we are really talking about, particularly when it comes to **the primary feeling state**, the most important experience of all.

Did you even know there was a different way of thinking than the linearity you have been taught? You are, of course, not the only one that didn't know. For a number of historical reasons, we've adroitly and convincingly avoided understanding that there is a completely different and *non*-linear way of thinking. It has made our supposed advanced technological civilization far, far from as "advanced" as it would otherwise be, however. The biggest things the insistence on linearity made us give up were innovation and solving problems.

In their extensive research for **"The First Idea, How Symbols, Language and Intelligence Evolved from Our Primate Ancestors to Modern Humans,"** doctors Greenspan and Shanker make it clear that the key is entirely in affect/emotion (p. 101):

> ...there is no algorithm, computer program or scientifically validated biological mechanism to explain complex human symbolic and reflective thinking. The problem here, however, is not that technology has not evolved far enough to

answer this age-old question of how we develop our higher-level reflective skills. **The problem is that for over four hundred years, Western thought has been drawn to a hypothesis that, at present, not only has no scientific data behind it, but is not consistent with any known biological or physical mechanism.**

. . . No matter how much potential his brain may have, unless a child undergoes very specific types of *interactive affective experiences* that involve the successive *transformations of emotional experience* and that are the result of cultural practices forming the very core of our evolutionary history, that potential will not be realized in a traditional sense.
(Boldface and italics, ours.)

We've tried desperately to make up for the limitations in our thinking. In the "Information Age" we have seen repeated attempts—prettily phrased, to be sure—to make unique innovations or exceptional solutions somehow magically appear from tired commodities, worn-out processes, stale ideas and useless machinations. It will never happen, but people keep trying because they are just not aware there is another way of thinking and producing.

Corporations and consultants talk and talk about their innovation "pipelines" as if such a thing could actually work, and about their "problem analyses" as if they could produce anything at all. Don't hold your breath. You cannot go into a tired, re-hashed process—dressed up in all kinds of official-sounding, business-like terminology, to be sure—and come out of it with a spectacular result, ever.

In "**The Gutenberg Galaxy**" in 1962, (p. 266) Marshall McLuhan, who for decades carefully studied the effects of literacy and linearity, remarked on exactly this—how **"linear, fragmented analysis" has a "remorseless power of homogenization."** There is no escaping it. *No matter what you do, you are going to produce the garbage of sameness.* In Spanish, there is an expression that says, *"Aunque la mona se vista de seda, mona se queda."* Which means, you may dress up the monkey in silks, but she's still going to be a monkey. Linearity produces sameness, homogenization, and commoditization...*only*.

We think it's for one of two reasons: either they try for so hard and for so long—the myth of "hard work" is the one myth that will never die—that finally, years and hundreds of attempts later, some small indicator gets produced accidentally, completely outside of their awareness; OR, they just give up and use nomenclature and linguistic gymnastics to cover their failure. Because *as far as innovation goes, there is failure everywhere.* Look around! Bad enough that projects fail—don't even consider innovation!

So let's make something fundamental very clear from the outset of this section: **INNOVATION IS EASY. PROBLEM-SOLVING IS EASY.** Except that neither will work if you go looking for them in the trash bin and in both cases, *waking consciousness is the trash bin.*

Can we say this any clearer? Until there is meaningful interaction between waking consciousness (linearity) and the non-conscious mind (non-linearity), you will get nowhere. Like many, you may pretend you have something when you really do not. We hope not, when innovating is so easy! It must offend the conscious sense of control, of immediate cause-and-effect, of being "master of the house" that so many people refuse to let go otherwise. Maybe if they tire enough, after years of getting nothing and resigning themselves to failure and loss, they might finally think— there has to be another way!

Or maybe, the idea of resorting to "mere" *feeling* is so offensive to some people that they refuse to go that route. If so, then they don't understand that **innovations and exceptional solutions take up so much bandwidth that they can't be expressed or produced or communicated in the meager, drip-by-drip, piecemeal chokehold of waking consciousness.** That's why we have a *non*-conscious mind. Our waking consciousness can't even handle listening to more than one conversation at a time!

This chapter is the opposite of the previous, where the facts of sameness, duplication, commoditization and "normalcy" were clarified as based on tiny fragments, in sequence. Step back. In the big picture, we live in a universe with endless, infinitely diverse possibilities. Do you want solutions or innovations that are somehow *the same* as something that already exists? Do you not believe in the infinite capabilities of the universe to generate something that never before existed?

In not understanding the infinity of diversity, despite our supposed technological advancement, we look like very primitive cultures that worship sameness as an expression of safety. Less than a hundred years ago, before Edwin Hubble, we thought the Milky Way was the only existing galaxy in the entire universe. The only one! Right up to January, 1930! We did however, wonder about those billions and billions of tiny, oval stars... They turned out, each one of them, to be entire, unique, previously unknown galaxies. You think that innovation you've been wanting isn't also right there, under your nose?

Be Clear About Your Role

It is not your job to do "hard work." Your efforts will be wasted. It's not your job to come up with the specific, new idea. Those belong to the role of the non-conscious. If you attempt to carry out those mistaken roles, you will severely delay or completely misguide what you are doing. You can see that the primary challenge, in recruiting the non-conscious mind to your service isn't in asking that it do the "wrong" thing, it's in asking that it do (in most cases) *anything at all!*

So you may ask yourself, "How do I communicate with the seemingly elusive, truly ineffable, non-conscious mind?! Well, the answer to that is always the same but you may forget what it is: communicate in its own language, and only in its own language, the language of feeling. And here you have two clear choices.

First, we'll document the major things to know about non-linearity, then we'll go over them again later with greater detail.

Genius consists of the ability to move between waking consciousness and the non-conscious mind with enough ease that there is an interplay between the two. That interplay provides the knowledge you need to accomplish what you want.

1. **Non-linearity is feeling**. We use different names for it in different situations, but they are all based on feeling: intuition, gut-feel, inspiration and insight. Genius detects and then resolves as necessary.

2. **Feeling is the single most fundamental human experience** there is. Everyone feels, all the time, except people that have worked to de-sensitize

themselves from feeling anything; desensitization is either based on denial beliefs or substances that induce it.

3. **You are feeling something right now**. It may be indifference, confusion, interest, boredom, excitement, but whatever it is, you are feeling something right now. You cannot *not* feel. Expanding your connection with your non-conscious mind depends on these perceptions.

4. **Feeling is knowing**. Feeling isn't linear, like information. It isn't formed from sequential fragments or any natural language or math or code. Feeling is instantaneous and complete—non-linear. You get the whole thing all at once. You don't wait to get to the end of the sentence or fragment or book or equation or spread sheet.

5. **Feeling is whole**; it contains all of its context in itself, as opposed to linearity, which can never communicate all its context and is therefore always incomplete.

6. **Feeling is not a commodity**, like information. **It's idiosyncratic**. It's unique to the person that has the feeling. Since it isn't digital it can't be reproduced or stored in that way. This is one of the hardest things for people to understand.

7. **Feeling is based on a particular individual's life history** and is part of a dynamic, life-long "language" of experiences. All experience is based on feeling.

8. **Feeling is energy**. The other sources of energy for our bodies—food, oxygen—are tangential to feeling. You don't get particularly hungry if you feel hopeless.

9. Other people will refuse to believe that feeling is knowing, or that feeling is knowledge. **Western culture has denigrated**, denied, diminished and dismissed feeling consistently and continuously for over a thousand years.

10. **All supposedly "rational" thinking is nevertheless based on feeling**. Western culture's denigration of feeling is based on believing that rationality(or logic, lucidity, etc.) is devoid of feeling, which modern technology has shown, and continues to show, is all made up. The brain can't make "rational" decisions *without* feeling.

11. Because they don't understand it and especially not how to use it, **many people are afraid of feeling anything**—although they can't avoid it—because they think of feeling, especially of feeling anything deeply, as out of their control, which is not true.

12. **It takes a certain dedication and discipline, plus the acceptance of certain beliefs, to take control of feeling and use it deliberately**, something Geniuses manage to learn, either because they had a role model or they intuited it for or some other reason.

And now, let's examine these in greater detail.

1. Non-linearity is feeling. We use different names for it in different situations, but they are all based on feeling: intuition, gut-feel, inspiration, all perceptions that are unique to an individual.

Why is feeling *non-* linear? Feeling has no fragments. There are no parts to a feeling; all feelings are whole in themselves. Since there are no parts, feelings have no sequence and thus, no waiting to understand the whole.

There is no other communication we can experience as human beings that is complete like this. Linearity, as you know, is always incomplete. Feeling is always whole. That's why information (in-formation) is always incomplete, while knowledge is always whole.

2. You are feeling something right now. Whether or not you believe that evolution gave you feeling as a continuous resource, or if you believe, as people have been taught by the culture, that feeling is extraneous and makes no sense, either way you are feeling something right now. That feeling is there for a purpose, whether you want it or not. Dismiss it and you will churn out mediocre results because you'll be unaware of how much you are not knowing. Genius is only possible with the participations of the non-conscious and that comes through with feeling.

3. Feeling is knowing. When you feel something strongly, can anyone tell you that you aren't? When you know something at a feeling level, you KNOW it. It becomes undeniable. Feeling what you know isn't informational; it isn't trivia and it isn't just data in-formation. Whatever you feel, you *know*.

What Thomas Kuhn called "normal science," in his book on **"The Structure of Scientific Revolutions,"** adheres rigidly to what we *already* know and it wants you to do the same. There is a scientific establishment that wants you define what is acceptable for you to know, which it will determine for you.

In the evolution of knowledge in human society today, that is a primitive point of view based mainly on the desire to control people. Ironic, because in extremely primitive, non-technological societies, it is the linearity of waking consciousness that gets little attention while the non-conscious mind is recognized, variously as god or spirituality or a higher force of some kind.

This is fitting in a way, in an era that is focused on creating commodities and "fixing" the abnormalities. Human beings can't escape that avalanche—we too are asked to be the same as everyone else, and that includes what we can and cannot know.

Except that this is where the Information Age's values come crashing down. Human beings are relentlessly idiosyncratic, but different in ways we hardly even know because our focus remains on the sameness, not on the differences. Still, the Information Age has a powerful desire for innovation—"what's the next big thing?"

You can't have it both ways—on the one hand, denying the value of idiosyncrasy and **decrying people's right to know** what they, individually and as a result of their life experiences, can *know*; and on the other hand, demanding innovation in the face of this.

This is the single greatest mystery of the Information Age: **individual idiosyncrasy and innovation** versus **mass commoditization and conformity**.

That *feeling is know ing* doesn't mean that other people have to have anything to do with what *you* know; it's only our need for controlling how people think that demands that. Knowing is not a commodity, despite all the hype and insistence on so-called "knowledge management," which being digital is of course based on commoditization and conformity.

What you *know* is yours intimately and is produced by you—by your non-conscious mind, which is the true source of innovation (new ideas that are right for you right now, and for your situation). Knowledge is either a one-size-fits-all commodity (in which case it is actually in-formation and *not* knowledge) or it is purely and deeply idiosyncratic. You cannot have it both ways without contradiction.

5. That feeling is whole means that feeling comes from such depths in *your experience*, that as you feel, you always "get it." There is no looking it up on Google to find out if it's a positive or negative feeling, or to find out if it's related to x or y or z. You already know. If you think you don't know, then you just check your insides and if you know how to "read" yourself, you will know. You may have to wait during a brief "gestation" period for an answer to a question, or for an idea, or for a solution, but once you get it, it comes as a feeling first—as intuition or inspiration—and then, it's undeniable and requires no explanations. When it "feels right" that's usually because it is.

6. What does it mean that feeling is not a commodity? Well, for one thing, it can't be directly copied and distributed, or saved on a server. Feeling isn't digital and linear and it isn't static. Information is always static. Information is just going to sit there, imprecise and incomplete where you last left it, until you go back and add or subtract or edit the data. In the meantime, there is nothing growing in it, there is nothing developing in it, there is nothing expanding in it. At all.

Knowledge as feeling is dynamic *all on its own*, because your non-conscious mind is busy at work on it. When you go back to the feeling and hold it inside you, it expands and becomes something newer, bigger, more meaningful. *That's why you pursue feeling.* That's how Geniuses get their big ideas. They pursue them and make them more and more meaningful. Eventually you figure out how other people can also *know* them, but you can never predict just how that will come about. Feeling is idiosyncratic in every way.

For a culture steeped in the value of sameness, commoditization and "normality," this is initially hard to understand. Diversity, differences, freakiness, the odd and unusual, the out-of-step, the abnormal, the-out-of-touch, the unexplainable, the quirky, the supposed failures, the undefinable—this is where the gold is. If you can't appreciate it you'll never get there because you won't know it when it appears. You may even depreciate and deny it.

7. What you feel comes from your own life history, from the beliefs that you have developed and from your aspirations because the energy that fuels positive feelings comes from desire. Desire is the fuel for everything we do and ultimately—this is something that science has conveniently "forgotten," although it was the result of extensive scientific research and experimentation over decades, with control groups, documentation, recording and all the processes of science—we know scientifically, thanks to social motivation psychology, that anything anyone wants is at its most clear and fundamental, *a desire for a feeling state.* **Whether you want your lucky number to come up or want a mansion or a promotion, you want it because you believe that if you have it,** *you will feel good* **or that** *you will feel better.*

Your non-conscious knows this in great detail. Do you not think that the same non-conscious mind that is *right now*, filtering your blood through your kidneys, digesting your lunch, managing your hormonal and endocrine systems, pulling oxygen into your bloodstream from your lungs, using white blood cells to defend your health—and on and on, all of which require intelligent decisions and billions of them each moment—is *not* intimately aware of what you want and registering it as it changes and expands, moment by moment!?

When your non-conscious mind communicates with you using the vast language of feeling, it is communicating instantaneously based on a complexity of inputs and records that you cannot begin to imagine with waking consciousness. We are much bigger than we know, but our insistence on the illusion of direct control keeps us small.

8. Feeling is energy. This is particularly easy to recognize and to prove for yourself. Just examine when it is that you feel greater energy in your body; is it when you are excited about what you're doing or when you are bored, irritated or distracted? How does your energy actually increase, when you feel happy and are about to do something you like or when you feel negative (there's a reason we call it "depression") and don't want to do what you are setting out to do?

If you want to energize a group, don't resort to hype, to theatrics or to bombast. Just ask them what they want to do and where they find that in their own work. The "engagement" of the workforce is not about activities— that's putting things backwards—it's about a *feeling*, which can then generate activities that keep expanding it. That feeling is also the primary mental state the invites new ideas in.

9. Some people will refuse to believe that feeling is knowing because it can be hard to buck a current that has been flowing throughout Western culture for over a thousand years. Fortunately for you as a project manager, people don't have to know how you do what you do!

Scientists go out of their way to avoid using what we sometimes call "the f-word," *feeling*, because it has been denigrated as unworthy of scientific research for so long. Now that we have technology that can get data as the brain actually functions, we are beginning to realize what cannot be denied: that feeling is essential to higher-order processes in the brain.

10. "Rational" thinking is still based on feeling. For an excellent source to begin understanding this, we recommend Antonio Damasio's **"Descartes' Error,"** which is precisely on this topic. Feeling as knowledge is the future and it's coming fast—we have ignored what has been right in front of our noses; there are far too many phenomena this explains that we couldn't explain before at all. Most of the research discoveries have been around for a long time, particularly the differences in capacity between waking consciousness and the non-conscious—undeniable, easily proven, yet roundly ignored as if waking consciousness could do much of anything beyond focusing, which demands all the bandwidth and intellect it has.

11. Because they don't understand it and especially not how to use it, **many people are afraid of feeling anything**—although they can't avoid it—because they think of feeling, especially of feeling anything deeply, as out of their control or something that might take control of them. This isn't as irrational as it may sound. If you don't understand the functions of feeling, you can feel like something else inside you is in control; it seems to make decisions without you. Actually, they *are* your decisions because they are based on beliefs you accepted long ago.

It's another one of those paradoxes of Genius. You have to give up short-term and immediate control and cause-and-effect to get a larger span of control when you pursue feeling. The non-conscious does not make decisions for the conscious mind, it just puts things together in ways that seem breath-taking to us. We interpret this as decisions that are made without us, when in reality, they are based on desires, values and decisions we can't even remember ever having made. You may have had a fleeting imagining of something that was dear to you fifteen years ago—do you think your non-conscious just dropped it and moved on? Not so!

12. Genius is about deliberately initiating and continuing the interplay between waking consciousness and the non-conscious for what together they can give us: the first gives us intimate and fundamental decisions about what we want; the other gives us the unique, personal knowledge that gets us there.

The Vocabulary for a Language without Words

All of the phenomena we're going to describe are easy to generate and very generous in what they give you in return. We are using words, which are *linear*, to describe *mental feeling states*, which are *non-linear*, which means that your own experience of them will ultimately be unique to you.

This gives the lie to knowledge as a digital commodity. Nothing can be more intimate and more a reality as knowledge than knowing how you feel. Feeling is knowledge. Everything else is just more information.

Intro-**spection** just means answering the question "how am I feeling right now?" an answer you can only get from your own insides. No one else can know this for you.

Imagination is just a way to ask for details regarding your most important question, "what do I want?" Your imagination will surprise you by offering unexpected choices as well as revealing beliefs you held but may not have been aware of. Those beliefs are in the reactions you find yourself having to what you are imagining, e.g., "That's not going to be possible!" "This is going to be fun!"

Intuition, Insight and Inspiration are *ways in which the non-conscious sends you knowledge*, the *ways in which the non-conscious speaks to you*. The objective of interplay with the non-conscious mind is precisely to generate these particular feelings which are knowledge.

You learn to understand and trust them, by trusting them; by experimenting with the idiosyncrasies of your own non-conscious, until they become second nature.

All of these involve energy because **feeling always involves energy**, no matter whether it's positive or negative. Words are an attempt to communicate that particular knowledge and energy. When the words do carry energy, they are attractive. When they don't, no matter how much meaning they may have, they are dead. There are adjectives we use words to describe people who can communicate *with feeling* (charismatic, powerful, articulate, convincing, influential, etc.) and those who communicate *without much feeling* (boring, disconnected, lackluster, rambling, nonsensical, etc.). Mostly we all do both. When the feeling is genuine, that experience can keep growing. When it's hype, then not so much.

You can also easily tell when someone is attempting to inject energy into their words, but that energy isn't genuine; it's forced or "evangelized." It may at first appear convincing, but it isn't sustainable. We see this in salespeople all the time, attempting to win over a sale with their "pumped up," fake high energy. Most sales forces don't understand that they have to first convince themselves with complete integrity, before they can convince someone else. When you understand feeling it's easy to detect a lie.

Identity is the sum result of what (you didn't know) you are creating over the course of your life, because building the capacity for Genius also happens to be the way you *build the "you" that you always wanted to be.* You don't really have to be concerned about it because it's mostly going to happen outside your awareness anyway, and revealed to you if and when you care to see it.

Intuition, Insight, "Gut-Feel" are moments of communication. Imagine how powerful the non-conscious is, that it can provide you with knowing in just an instant, and in that instant make completely clear situations so complex and so saturated with context that the world changes for you.

These are the **lightning flashes of intuition** through which a new paradigm is born" that Kuhn is referring to ("**The Structure of Scientific Revolutions**"). When you construct a question or request for knowledge on a particular topic, once practiced, the non-conscious will meet your request with an intuitive or insightful "flash." That flash is *knowing*.

Inspiration is no different. Organizations worry about employee "engagement" and offer all kinds of activities to build teamwork and expand engagement, not understanding that engagement is a feeling, not an activity. It is a feeling that can generate all kinds of discretionary energy and activity, but the activity part comes second, as a consequence of the feeling. If you can't address feeling as a part of the organization's internal climate, then taking about engagement is useless.

Inspiration is positive energy in the direction of an outcome. If you address the outcome with a lot of activity (working hard) without addressing the feeling *first*, then the activity will only have limited results because it will have limited energy and few ideas. It's the difference between acting after breathing in, versus acting while holding your breath. Inspiration needs to be continuously cultivated and this is done through **appreciation** of everything related to the project that you can perceive as *good*.

The Primary Feeling State

The primary feeling state for accessing the non-conscious mind is simple: it's a state of mind in which you feel content, happy, relaxed, and joyous or their equivalents. In sum, you feel good. That is the only mental state that opens the non-conscious to interplay with waking consciousness. It's physics: a question of mental bandwidth.

Why? The non-conscious mind will not respond to stress, which is the general term for *not* feeling good and other forms of hell. When you are stressed, your waking consciousness is deeply engaged with a specific negative idea. The only way to eliminate the interference of stress is to focus on its opposite, *feeling good*. When you don't do this and engage the stress, waking consciousness is saying to the non-conscious mind, "not now! Don't provide me with great solutions or innovations right now—I'm too busy focusing on feeling stressing out!" It's not the non-conscious mind that is refusing to cooperate; it's waking consciousness because it wants to be in charge, even if that means going down with the ship.

Why? Waking consciousness gets fully focused with any amount of stress. Remember, it has very little bandwidth, so there's never any to spare. Focus is its purpose, as long as you allow it. There are some things that it's good to be focused on and others that it's not.

When you are under stress you *cannot* get great new ideas. It is physically not possible. Stress is a powerful trigger for waking consciousness; when you are examining reality from that perspective, the door is closed on the non-conscious mind.

The non-conscious only communicates with the broad bandwidth of feeling, addressing issues with a depth and meaning that consciousness cannot. The non-conscious cannot focus on waking consciousness' stress. Focusing is not its job; it sees the big picture, not the specific negative. The boiler burst. The project won't make the deadline. My car won't start. The client is complaining about x, etc.

Granted, you can't get from stress directly to singing in the rain.

Negative specifics are where feeling bad comes from. You can transform them.

There are a number of iconic tales about famous scientists and mathematicians coming up with their theories while they are in a relaxed, physical and mental state: Sir Francis Newton, looking out the window and seeing an apple fall, was inspired with questions that led to his theory of gravitation; Archimedes of Syracuse, greatest of the ancient mathematicians, came up with his theory about the displacement of water as he stepped into a bath, and so on.

We have mentioned that waking consciousness has the exceptional, fundamental and primary ability of **focus**. Focus can generate wonderful results, but it can also generate disastrous ones. The good news is that if you know how it works, you can choose—that's focus right there. **Focus allows for choosing what you want at any moment,** consciousness' only real function and something the non-conscious mind cannot and does not do.

Sometimes you are so stressed, angry, depressed or despairing that you can't get to feeling good, but you can get to *feeling somewhat better.* That becomes the job, because how you feel can change if you go about it in increments.

When you are not feeling good, that only means that you are focused on something you don't really want and your non-conscious is making that point for you. "Hey! What are you doing? That's not what you want! Hello? Remember me?"

Negative feelings are always about something *specific* that your waking consciousness is choosing to focus on, **something negative and specific**. (E.g., "When is this group ever going to cooperate?!" "The numbers don't add up!")

When your non-conscious mind communicates to you with a negative feeling, it can only mean one thing: no!; stop!; this isn't it!; look elsewhere!; do something different!; step back!

The best ways to get to the primary mental state of feeling good or feeling better are: **go to an abstraction or generalization that applies to the situation** (e.g., "The truth is that groups like this always come around and end up being supportive..." or "I'll figure this out; I always do.") or, if you can, **appreciate the things that are going well**, that you do feel good about (e.g., "The truth is I love this job and I've had a great year already.").

As a Genius you become an expert at regularly transforming the negative and specific into the positive and abstract.

Why do this? Because when you are under stress, there is something that you want, and whatever you want requires a new perspective or a new idea; you need a different, positive feeling state so that those are possible. You want to get into your primary mental state.

We call that mental state the "primary mental state" because it is your *optimal* mental state. You can't sustain it continuously. If you could, you would never be creatively *desiring*—it takes obstacles to generate desire—but you *can* evoke it and keep yourself there much more often than you know.

Geniuses know how to do this. That's why they can be so predictably creative. You now have their major secret! That's why in the middle of a nightmare situation, Geniuses have taught themselves to relax, or at least, to feel better than the other people who are running around screaming and freaking out.

What are Geniuses feeling good about?

Geniuses feel good about themselves; about their aspirations; about watching their ideas develop; about generating new ideas all the time; about seeing things that others do not; about the easy joys of thinking, whenever or wherever they want; about their past successes, however insignificant they may seem to others; about extending their own capabilities in the arenas they love; about producing, seemingly effortlessly; about knowing what other people do not; about watching their own identity grow and evolve; about constantly learning about themselves; about abandoning "working hard" in favor of enjoying what they do; about their burgeoning self-confidence and feeling of worthiness; about wanting new ideas on a topic and in short order, having them appear...

Any form of stress is the opposite mental state from the primary mental state. The deleterious effects of stress have been studied over and over for decades. Today, studies on the effects of stress are published annually in articles and books by the thousands.

Here are two we identified this very week, while editing this document:

- **"The science of forgiveness: When you don't forgive you release all the chemicals of the stress response"** and

- **"Working longer hours increases stroke risk by up to 33%: study."**

These are truly random selections; we chose them as the first two we came across, only upon doing the final edits to these (incomplete for this purpose) pages. Then we added the following observations.

The first was published on **salon.com**; the second, on **yahoo.com/news**, both in early September, 2015.

The first article is based on studies carried out mainly with burn victims and addresses the difference that changing how they interpreted and felt about what they experienced, fundamentally changed their medical prospects. It is based on rigorous scientific studies carried out at a number of universities with hospitals.

Here are some of the conclusions:

> 'When you don't forgive you release all the chemicals of the stress response,' Luskin says. 'Each time you react, adrenaline, cortisol, and norepinephrine enter the body. When it's a chronic grudge, you could think about it twenty times a day, and **those chemicals limit creativity, they limit problem-solving**. Cortisol and norepinephrine cause your brain to enter what we call 'the no-thinking zone,' and

over time, they lead you to feel helpless and like a victim. When you forgive, you wipe all of that clean.' [Boldface ours.]

[From **"Triumph of the Heart: Forgiveness in an Unforgiving World"** by Megan Feldman Bettencourt. Published by arrangement with Avery, an imprint of Penguin Publishing Group, a division of Penguin Random House LLC. Copyright © 2015 by Megan Feldman Bettencourt.]

We would add, it's not that they "limit" creativity and problem-solving, it's that *they make them altogether impossible*. It really is, as the article states, a "no-thinking zone."

Brain neuroscience has accomplished more in the last 20 years than in all previous human history. However, our concern isn't the particular chemicals involved in these processes. Rather, it is the fact that stress—in the case of the article, severe injury—closes access to feeling good, *if you don't address it*. When you are focused on the stress—remember that *focus* is waking consciousness' premier capability—you cannot access the non-conscious and its potential gifts, because you cannot access the primary feeling state that opens the doors.

The second article we mentioned, **"Working longer hours increases stroke risk by up to 33%: study,"** addresses a series of studies on this topic, and one particular detail:

> "In looking at the link between long hours in the work place and heart disease", Mika Kivimaki, a professor of epidemiology at University College London, and colleagues analyzed data from 25 studies involving 603,838 men and women from Europe, the

United States, and Australia who were followed for an average of 8.5 years... 'The pooling of all available studies on this topic allowed us to investigate the association between working hours and cardiovascular disease risk with greater precision than has previously been possible,' Kivimaki said in a statement.

'Health professionals should be aware that working long hours is associated with a significantly increased risk of stroke, and perhaps also coronary heart disease.'

Working long hours is "associated" with the stress but it isn't the cause. The stress is provoked because you are doing something you don't want to do. If you were doing something you were passionate, excited about, it wouldn't be hard work; it would be pleasurable and invigorating. It would *improve your health!*

Studies on stress are a field day for researchers because there are so many causes to investigate. On the other hand, there are studies on feeling good that prove undeniable positive effects, as in the previous article. What neither field of research is making clear is our main thesis in this book: that **how you feel has a powerful impact on the "conversation" with the non-conscious mind: stress closes it off completely, while feeling good opens it up.**

Geniuses depend on that internal conversation.

How Do You "Work *Smarter,* Not *Harder?*" and the Enduring Myth of "Hard Work"

Geniuses work smarter, but when someone says this to you they only say it because in that moment they know what they *think* you should be doing. No one will ever say, "I don't know how you can do this, but worker smarter, not harder."

Working smarter means using a great idea, but no one can tell you how to come up with an idea specific to what you need. They're certainly not going to tell you that to come up with the idea, you have to stop what you're doing!

Here's why people think that thinking is a waste of time, and that action! action! action! should always be the imperative:
At first, people *think* that waking consciousness can come up with great new ideas because waking consciousness is restless, but they don't understand that there is a VAST difference between coming up with *an idea—any* idea—and *the great new idea you need.*

The first is the new idea that is just *more* information, *more* trivia, *more* context, *more* linearity. Yes, it may be "new" only because you just thought it up, but so what? You have no feeling for it. The second is genuine knowledge of the person and the situation; it has energy in feeling. They exist in two different universes that we are never taught to distinguish. So people get discouraged and then give up on thinking and resign themselves to *really hard work.*

Have you noticed that self-proclaimed gurus of innovation always tell you that innovation—which just means coming up with *a great idea for a specific situation*—is "really, really hard!" It isn't at all, but they don't know how to do that and they do know this: that if you have enough desire and try long enough, *something* may come about much later!

That's still hard work and a waste of time and (forced) energy.

Hard work is never about the work itself, it's about *how you feel about the work*. The very same activity can be a burden or it can be enjoyable; perspective is everything. There is often someone that would enjoy doing what you might consider hard work that you don't want to do.

Hard work is never about extreme physical labor, at least not in the 21st century. Just how does one work hard? Putting in longer hours? Working with one hand tied behind your back? Working while blind-folded? Wearing a hair shirt while working? **Hard work is a mental state** and one of the many ridiculous contradictions that linearity engenders: you have the *desire* to produce something but *you do not want to do it* in the only way you can think of doing it! How does that *not* require a new idea?

Work is hard when you really don't want to do it. Most people feel they can't be honest about this because they have no choice, which is never true. There is always something *less hard*, an *easier* alternative, if you have a different, new perspective or a new idea. Of course, if you aren't feeling good or can't get yourself to at least feeling *better*, you won't get the new perspective you need because you shut the mental doors to input from your non-conscious mind. First, you have to be in a mental state we call *the primary mental state*—more on that later. Hard work always calls for a new perspective, a new idea. Since we don't think we can generate those easily, we do the hard work.

Hard work is always linear. It's a myopic, fragmented view of reality but your waking consciousness doesn't have enough bandwidth to see that. It is challenging to let go of hard work because there are so many rewards for "effort," whether you succeed or not.

Remember the expression, "You get an 'A' for effort"? That means, "You worked really hard and didn't produce anything, but I still approve of you." Much of what we do is defined around how we want other people to see us and not on what we really want. What you really want when doing hard work, is to be able to turn your attention to something you enjoy that also produces results that you want.

Have you noticed that initially at least, hard work is visible and noticed by other people? That's why it involves some sort of physical effort. You don't dare leave the office at 3:30; you want the boss to see you leave at 7:00—or at least to think you did. We do hard work mainly to impress others and prove we are worthy.

Unfortunately, over time most work becomes hard work even when no one else can see it; it becomes the only way to think about work. **This is how hard work creates more hard work.** If *you* aren't ensuring that you are doing work that you are passionate about, who can ensure that for you? Who is going to create the enjoyable life of fulfillment, accomplishment and recognition that you want for yourself?

The contrast between linearity and non-linearity always produces paradoxes: **the most productive work you can do is not immediately visible to other people**—one of the many reasons Geniuses can't pay attention to what other people think. You have to sit down and think and feel carefully.

When faced with a huge challenge, problem or opportunity, what do you do first?

If you are thinking (and used to thinking) in linear terms, you roll up your sleeves! Nose to the grindstone! Tote that barge; lift that bale! Drink 17 energy drinks!

Geniuses proceed differently and in ways others can't see they're doing. It's a simple process that involves almost everything Geniuses do.

FIRST, they always begin by checking their insides to see how they feel about the whole thing. Their feeling about it is knowledge that is important to them.

SECOND, they determine if they are feeling bad or good about it, because it's going to be one or the other. As we said, that feeling is knowledge, whichever it is.

THIRD, they stay in, or move to, the primary feeling state as much as possible, until they get an inspiration, an intuition, an idea about what to actually do. That's knowledge too.

It takes practice to make this a habit, of course. This is a *physical* process, not just a thinking process. When you learn to skateboard, it's not by reading a book about skateboarding. You have to get on the thing and give it a try, over and over, and *feel it* get easier. **Experience is always a feeling or a lot of perceptions, sensations and feelings.**

Hard work is actually lazy because it always precludes what should come *first* but gets avoided: an exploration into how you're feeling about the situation contrasted with what you really want . . . which is all the thinking people prefer to avoid because they don't understand it.

The productive work is the thinking/feeling that will actually generate a new idea, not the hard work you don't want to do. When you do it this way and get the idea you wanted, then you're not really "working" and certainly not "hard" because you are fueled by interest, by happiness at getting the idea, even by excitement or passion. In that idea, you have created something as a Genius, and Genius is always about creating.

When people ask someone else . . .

- "How can I get all this done in time?"
- "This is so complicated; how will I do it?"

- "Nobody's ever accomplished this. What can I do?"

- "How did you ever do this?"

- "How did you come up with the idea for...?"

- "I'm overwhelmed. What can I do?"

. . . What they typically get in response is "you have to work really hard."
What people are *really* saying with that answer, is "I don't really know how you can get this done." Or, "I don't really know what you can do when you're overwhelmed."

There are several world-famous, clearly successful entrepreneurs we've heard say this in interviews on television. They don't have a clue as to how they were inspired at different points in their lives or how they got so "lucky," or got to feeling so passionate, or developed their idea in the first place, so when asked how they achieved success, they respond "I worked really hard." That is the socially accepted answer, but it says exactly nothing.

People honestly don't know, but don't want to appear stupid or clueless. The truth is when it comes to their use of feeling (intuition, inspiration, innovation, etc.) they have no idea. If they said, "I got inspired" or "I generated a new idea," then you would reasonably ask, "how did you do that?" and they wouldn't know what to say to that either. So here's the translation no one ever explained to you before: **"hard work" really means "I don't know."**

Faced with hard work (work that you do not feel passionate about and don't really want to do) the challenge is to innovate, to get a different perspective, to come up with a new idea. We'll explain further how to do this. As we say repeatedly regarding hard work, Geniuses aren't martyrs and martyrs aren't Geniuses. To address this and any obstacle, you need to get yourself into what we call **the primary feeling state.** Geniuses aren't martyrs and martyrs aren't Geniuses.

Self-Talk: Why Genius Project Managers Love Talking to Themselves

This is one of a Genius' most important functions, and although we don't like computer analogies for human beings, we'll use this one: Genius project managers "re-program" themselves from the useless or even counter-productive ideas and beliefs that can sabotage what they want, through self-talk. As we've mentioned, they can discover them in the first place, using their imagination of future events.

Self-talk is a profoundly important tool. You might think that because it's called "talk" that it has to do with words, but it actually has little to do with words and a lot to do with feeling. The words are just a conveyance device. You focus on the feeling you are pursuing and use words to get you there.

Geniuses often "check in" with how they are feeling. It's a gut level thing, and when you do, you find you are either feeling good or not so good; you are in the primary feelings state or you are not. An additional reason for doing this is that when you do, you may also have an idea "come to mind," as an intuition or simply what we call "gut feel," if you're feeling good. Geniuses stay in touch with that part of their bodies throughout the day. It's a reading device for how they are doing at any particular moment. It's also great to feel good!

We cannot forget, and so we remind you over and over, that the single most important fact about how we think—not conjecture, but *proven fact*—is the importance of managing the difference between the roles of waking consciousness and the non-conscious mind, and self-talk is a way to do this.

Managing that difference is never included in the prescriptions, recommendations and explanations of "how to innovate" or "how to solve problems" by people who go into those topics—consultants, academics, gurus, advisors, counselors, mentors—yet without understanding that difference, innovating and problem solving are only guesswork, blind trial and error, or hopeful "hard work," with no *certainty* of finding a solution anywhere, ever. Norretranders "cuts consciousness down to size" at the same time that he expands our understanding of who we really are beyond waking consciousness...

> Subliminal perception and nonconscious mental activity mean that man's link to the world is far stronger than consciousness suspects. Leibniz knew this, and psychology knew it at the end of the nineteenth century. But the twentieth century has been a story of forgetting this link; of regarding consciousness as the

whole story of man's connection with the world.

Now the wind is changing, and people are again realizing that they are far more than they themselves can know. (Norretranders, p. 327).

Geniuses of course, know this full well. They don't just know it. They *know* it.

In "**The Mind and The Brain**, Schwartz and Begley make clear a connection between mental effort and material results in brain neurology: neuroplasticity. For their explanation, they go as far back as to the prescient philosopher and psychologist William James (1842–1910) and his work on volition in mental activity. Their explanation of the application of quantum physics to understanding these processes is powerful and clear, in what they call "mental force." It is, in our words, the application of focus to desire or feeling. They believe that it is a cause of neuroplasticity and that in this way, our deliberate thinking ends up changing the physical brain.

That is to say, Geniuses have neurologically different brains because they are going about changing them in their normal, daily thinking, not because they were born Geniuses, as some, including brain neurologists, would have us believe.

> Since attention is generally considered an internally generated state . . . **introspection, willed attention, subjective state**—pick your favorite description of an internal mental state— can redraw the contours of the mind, and in so doing can rewire the circuits of the brain, for it is attention that makes neuroplasticity possible. (Bodlface ours, p. 339).

Attention always involves some level of feeling because attention (focus) is a choice, and choices involve feeling, whether consciously or not. And, quoting from the work of Mike Merzenich and Rob deCharms on attention and volition, and referring to neuroplasticity:

> This leaves us with a clear physiological fact . . . **moment by moment we choose who we will be in the next moment in a very real sense,** and these choices are left embossed in physical form on our material selves. (Boldface ours, Ibid.)

And so, back to self-talk. Self-talk means choosing what you are paying attention to, and that choice, if it involves getting into the primary feelings state of feeling good (or of feeling better), means that you are deliberately opening the doors to the discoveries that the non-conscious mind—and only the non-conscious—can provide.

Geniuses aren't talking to themselves for the sake of merely talking; **they are talking themselves into a particular mental state.** It is purposeful, deliberate talk and it is often for moving from a specific negative, to a more abstract, generalized state of mind. Let's look at an invented example:

- "I'm not feeling great because our beta test was a complete failure."

- "Well, failures are part of the process."

- [After each declaration there an a *feeling* question that has to be answered before the next step: does this make me feel *better* or *worse?* If *better*, then continue. If *worse*, go back to another abstraction and try that.]

- "I've had failures before. I got myself through those, I can get myself through this one."

- "Besides, failure is relative. In the big picture of things, this is just a moment."
- "Let me go relax and forget about it for a while, and then think about all the undeniably great things we *have* accomplished so far..."

What we're insisting on that drives the desire to feel good isn't an *ethical* imperative, it's a *hedonistic* imperative. It is motivated by the love of creation, of generating new ideas, of solving problems, and of innovating because all of these *feel good* to the Genius.

Only Imagination Straddles Waking Consciousness *and* the Non-Conscious

Imagination is a very unique mind phenomenon, because it seems to straddle *both* waking consciousness *and* the non-conscious. First, let's clarify how prevalent it is and how we take it for granted.

We are all imagining every day, some people more than others. We have an idea, as the day begins and we are, say, getting dressed, about what the day will be like. We have imagined it. We also have at least an idea about what the week and month will be like. These are all products of our imaginations, usually extending outward in time what we already experience. That's partly why most people's lives don't change much—they expect to experience more of what they already are experiencing. That leads them to think and act in ways that produce exactly that.

Many people plan out far into the future and we're not talking just about mental planning on a calendar, but rather, thinking of the future with strong feelings, repeatedly. The reason Imagination straddles both waking consciousness and the non-conscious is because on the one hand, with regard to waking consciousness, *Imagination is a question of focus and choice* (even if it doesn't always seem that way) and we know that focus and choice are the primary functions of waking consciousness (or to put it more clearly, waking consciousness looks to answer the question, "What do you want?").

On the other hand, with regard to the non-conscious, Imagination can include the element of feeling, the language of the non-conscious. When you imagine something you really, really want, there are particularly strong feelings, just as there also are when you imagine something that you are expecting but dreading. Any form of *Expectation* is a form of

Imagination: creating ideas and feelings in your mind about a future event. The stronger your feelings about that future event, the more likely it becomes because of the energy that gets developed and that directs your thinking and behavior.

You can decide you want tomorrow to be an easy day for you, and you can imagine it in that way, generating lots of ideas for how that could be, without fixating on any particular one, but instead, fixating on the feeling of ease.

If you want something to happen but don't really expect it to—at a *feeling* level of expectation—which do you think is going to win out? That question becomes, where is the greatest energy, in the feeling of the desire or in the feeling of the expectation?

Of course, the interplay between the two forms of consciousness is continuous in our minds, even if we are not aware of it at all. But with Imagination, we have exceptional forces at our disposal for creating expectations that will direct our non-conscious in ways that we want. In many ways, Expectation and Imagination create our lives.

Imagination is the capacity to think of something that doesn't exist in material reality and to come up with mental images, concepts and feelings that confer on it a degree of reality that didn't exist before.

Imagination is often denigrated as day-dreaming and wasting time by those that don't understand that anything that exists in material reality began first in some form of consciousness, ***inside someone's head***. Your projects are first, an *idea* about a possible reality—the updated software, the new product prototype, the successful development process, the dreamed-of app, the enchanting song, the riveting movie, and so on. Project management takes ideas and turns them into a palpable, material reality. Project management is about creation and about innovation.

How does this happen?

It happens by applying energy to generating *more* ideas, ideas that are aligned with the Genius project manager's vision; ideas that add momentum, power, force, energy, ease, passion, dedication, excitement; ideas that expand beliefs and build conviction and connect resources; ideas that leverage other ideas; ideas that make the project clearly take off; ideas that make it begin to reveal its exciting, true nature; ideas that validate the formerly uncertain concepts and vision; ideas that win over people that were skeptical; ideas that increase ease and turn problems into novel solutions . . . and eventually, those *ideas upon ideas upon ideas and feelings upon feelings upon feelings*, all fully coalesce into one outcome and there you have it: the exceptionally successful, completed Genius of a project.

Any successful project is a creation of something new. A successful project is always an innovative process. It moves the intangible—an idea—into the material world. As with any phenomenon in physics, it takes energy to do this. That energy isn't gasoline; it isn't solar heat; it isn't from muscle and physical effort; that energy is generated from *feeling*—feelings that build deliberately and generate more ideas and more feeling.

Without the feeling, there would be a dearth of ideas. Feeling is knowing; ideas are generated by feeling. The Genius project manager's passion and vision of success snowball steadily and acquire definition, form, and reality. It becomes something you can see. It begins as something abstract, undefined, formless, and slowly, progressively, it comes into focus and into material reality.

Some of the most disastrous projects we've been asked to review in their aftermath are actually projects where people worked the hardest with regard to the hours they put in and the sacrifices they made. This is usually quite stunning for them to grasp. Our devotion to "hard work" is never given up easily! Martyrs aren't Geniuses; Geniuses aren't martyrs.

Imagination has a big role to play, especially in two respects: it provides a *vision* of the future and it lays clear the *belief systems* involved—both the ones that support it and the ones that don't.

The imagination is tied to *beliefs* because beliefs are the boundaries for understanding the reality we live in and those boundaries are malleable.

Geniuses daydream and imagine what they want, often. Open, relaxed imagining is one of the many mind-states that allow the non-conscious mind to communicate what it *knows* and also what it *believes*.

If you want to be a Genius, you need to cultivate the pleasure of thinking and of observing your thinking so you can learn from it. The more you cultivate it as a *pleasure*, rather than as an obligation, the easier and more rewarding it will become.

That represents the two purposes that imagination serves:

1. Your imagination helps you understand what it is that you really want and ultimately, it leads you to a vision of success. As you imagine, you will be asking yourself questions and reflecting on topics that would not have otherwise occurred to you and that are important to consider, especially *before* they make themselves an issue.

They will be produced in the way that the non-conscious mind often gets our attention: they *come to mind*. In this way, it is easier to embellish your own knowledge of what you want. That's something that you certainly can't get from a database, or from Google search... And if you've decided you really *do* want this new thing that has occurred to you, this new thing that has *come to mind*, then the question becomes, how do I want it to come about?—and so you imagine *that*.

Imagination and day-dreaming are infinitely productive, but the ways we think about them can make it difficult to accept that. It may be far more productive to sit and imagine, than to "*actually _do_ something*" because one of our beliefs about thinking at all is that when we engage in it, we aren't actually *doing* anything—the mistaken idea that effort is valuable for its own sake. "Work hard, it's good for you!" Geniuses don't engage in that constraint.

2. Imagination can show you the limits of what you *believe* about reality—the limits of what will be possible in your own reality. Beliefs, as we mentioned, are the boundaries of the realities we create for ourselves. If you don't believe that your project will succeed, for example, it will not succeed. Your non-conscious mind will make sure of it, that is, you'll sabotage yourself unwittingly.

Most unwitting sabotage happens with many small beliefs that go unattended, rather than with a large one like "this will never work. For example, you believe that the Compliance Department will never accept the project plan. Or that your boss will sink some of its ideas and not support it fully. If you believe those things strongly enough, then—surprise! The Compliance Department has sent you an urgent e-mail, and it's not a fun one. Oh, and also—your boss has called you into his office...

The non-conscious mind is endlessly creative, but it does not go beyond the boundaries of what we believe, ever. It *is* actually being creative, as it knows how to be, just not in the direction you want. Your stated hopes may be in a positive direction, but if your *feelings* are in another, feeling trumps everything else, every time. Feelings are energy.

The non-conscious mind doesn't initiate answers to the question of what we want, but sometimes it seems like it does, because it has such a long-term, wide-scope, seemingly universal view of all of our life, that it can piece together a reality that seems unexpected, but is just a lifetime of preferences, desires and aspirations we've forgotten. The non-conscious does not forget and never dismisses.

So, here we are at the boundaries of reality: our beliefs. In many so-called "post-mortems," examining the dead body of a project that ended badly, when the team members feel safe enough to be honest with each other, you will usually hear people say things like:

> "The truth is, I really didn't think this was going to work."
> "I suspected things were going wrong and I didn't think they would get resolved, but I sure didn't want to be the 'messenger!'"
> "I kept thinking that projects like this never succeed."
> "This was far too ambitious from the beginning. We weren't realistic."

These are all example of beliefs that limited the reality the project was attempting to create, defining the actual boundaries that people would end up acting on, whether they were conscious of it or not. The question is first, *identifying the beliefs*, and second, *changing them.*

The imagination works extremely well in *identifying* beliefs, because when you attempt to mentally create a reality that is at odds with your beliefs, *you'll feel it*.

Imagination also works extremely well in *changing* beliefs if you pursue the *feeling* that is at the heart of the new belief. If it's just words that you pursue, you'll get nothing.

The reason for pursuing, practicing, exercising, and getting to really *know* the feeling that really defines the new belief, which is because you want to build a "head of steam," energy, momentum, *more* feeling, initiative, desire...all of the forces that end up creating a reality. Creating reality can mean changing a belief, and that doesn't happen instantaneously.

You can't diminish a belief that you don't want by focusing on it or analyzing it; you have to move yourself to its opposite. If you analyze it or notice it in any way further, then it gathers steam which is exactly what you *don't* want. Beliefs are like ideas, they thrive grow and expand on the energy of attention, of focus—the primary function of waking consciousness. Beliefs can slip into it really easily, even when you don't want them to, if you aren't paying attention to how you feel.

Imagination is about "remembering the future" because it makes that future so real, building the ideas and the energy for it, that it—the intangible—becomes almost as real as the physical, and then suddenly—oh look!—it is!

In "**The Creating Brain**," a book that is mainly on the lives and accomplishments of particular Geniuses, psychiatrist Nancy C. Andreasen speculates briefly on the actual mental processes of Geniuses.

Unfortunately, she suggests that Geniuses are a type of privileged being with unique neurology or what she calls "special creatives." Sorry. Yes, practice changes the brain but everyone has the potential; Genius is not genetic. Although she does flirt with the idea of brain plasticity, the book doesn't make clear an essential fact we firmly believe: everyone has the capacity for Genius. Still, we want to quote one of her speculations to end this part of our book because her ideas on the unconscious processes involved is brilliant:

> These introspective accounts are describing a process during which thought is not only nonsequential or nonlinear, but during which nonrational unconscious processes play a role. It is as if the multiple association cortices are communicating back and forth, not in order to integrate associations with sensory or motor input as is often the case, but simply in response to one another. The associations are occurring freely. They are running unchecked, not subject to any of the reality principles that normally govern them. Initially these associations might seem meaningless or unconnected. I would hypothesize that during the creative process the brain begins by *disorganizing*, making links between shadowy forms of objects or symbols or words or remembered experiences that have not previously been linked. Out of this disorganization, self-organization eventually emerges and takes over in the brain. The result is a completely new and original thing: a mathematical function, a symphony, or a poem. (pp. 77-78).

...or, we would add, a great project, an unexpected innovation or a spectacular solution to an impossible problem.

III

How Do Geniuses Manage Projects?

To an observer, the practice of Geniuses is rife with paradoxes. For example...

Geniuses don't do much talking with *others*, but do lots of talking to *themselves*. They never ask for and don't generally listen to what others have to say about things, but the Genius insists on *mainly listening to others* rather than *speaking*. In particular settings, Geniuses listen to *others* in order to hear *themselves!* Geniuses *use* linear indicators and measures but don't *rely* on them at all. Geniuses aren't moved much by information but produce knowledge incessantly and value it enormously. Geniuses work in environments that are similar or the same as others' around them, but see things and know things about what's happening that those others do not. Geniuses' work is about *thinking*, but their methods are actually *physical*. Geniuses produce and create exceptionally, but never work hard. We could go on.

Paradoxes get generated when *two* forms of consciousness, that use two *different* languages and that see the world in fundamentally different (and often, opposed) ways, interplay with each other to create something.

Anything that you create without these two forms of consciousness interplaying will just be *mediocre* or *incremental* (adding to something that isn't innovated but that rather, already exists).

Paradoxes are inevitable, but they don't need resolution. They are their own resolution. Geniuses never have to stress about paradoxes at all because they know that in every instance, feeling leads. Desire and feeling trump everything else.

Getting to *Certainty*

Project management exists as a discipline to produce specific outcomes by controlling the processes for achieving those outcomes. In other words, **project management exists to generate specific outcomes with some measure of certainty**. The opposite of certainty is uncertainty or unpredictability.

When projects fail for any particular reason and this becomes finally clear, failure gets attributed to something "unpredictable" and the rationale is often, "how could we have *known*?" **Certainty is knowing.**

Certainty can't be measured and can't be guaranteed; ultimately it's a feeling—an important and abiding one when it's strong and genuine. We'll get back to that later. We are driving towards a very BIG change in how you understand project management, so we are taking this step by step.

What we call project management "methodology"—the pages and pages of recommendations, the pie charts, the measurement, the analogies to other systems, the hierarchies of procedures and processes, the dashboards, the nomenclature, the lessons learned, the best practices, the Gantt charts, the PowerPoint slides, the stages and other fragments, putting things in order from general to specific—we could go on and on—*are all <u>linear phenomena</u> measuring, relating, interpreting and generating <u>other linear phenomena</u>* (usually data of some kind).

If you can measure it *with only numbers or words*, it's linear. **Linear phenomena measuring *other* linear phenomena, of themselves, can only produce mediocrity.** They miss far too much of what's really going on.

When you look out into the world, what you see and feel isn't linear. As Nørretranders puts it:

> The balance between the linear and the nonlinear is a major challenge for civilization. In the final analysis, it is closely related to the challenge of finding the balance between the conscious and the nonconscious. After all, the difference between consciousness and nonconsciousness is precisely that **there is very little information in consciousness**. It can therefore apprehend only straight lines, having trouble with crooked ones, which contain far too much information. (Boldface, ours; p. 393).

Since projects are eminently linear, why wouldn't project managers, who are most solidly linear thinkers and who actively espouse linear processes and measurements, be the most successful?

Remember that "threshold skills," a concept developed by researchers rigorously assessing job competence during the 1970's, means *a skill that is needed for the job but that is an entry-level requirement and not evidence of superior performance.*

Threshold skills do not distinguish between superior-performance and average performance in a given job, no matter how good you are at them. Threshold skills are usually, in most jobs, entirely linear. The characteristics required to be successful in the job are always *non*-linear.

Project management theories may have an *approximation* to the anticipated situation that students and managers learn to address, but reality is always broader, more complex, more detailed and in sum, unpredictable enough that it cannot be covered completely by even the most elaborate theories and practices. Even the most highly touted "best practices" are bound to fail. Can we agree on this? This is the difference between theory and reality. Reality wins out every time—the 75%+ failure rate of projects testifies to the truth of this.

In **"The Competent Manager, A Model for Effective Performance,"** (1982) which is based on studies generated over decades, Richard Boyatzis clarified that it is not only entry-level information—the standardized processes and procedures you learned in management school—that are at the threshold level of competence; "threshold competence" also applies to the many forms of specialized knowledge that managers may use:

> This suggests that certain facts and concepts are needed by a manager to perform his or her job, but having more of the specialized knowledge does not by itself contribute to superior performance as compared to average performance in the job. In this sense, *specialized knowledge can be considered a threshold competency.*(p. 184).

Here is our first hypothesis regarding competence as a project manager:

Hypothesis No. 1: You cannot *go into* a project with linearity as your primary criteria—or what job competency analysis calls *threshold skills* (the *standardized* practices, methodologies, measurements, etc., that you'll learn from schools, books, certificate programs, PowerPoint presentations and other linear media, all of which are linear)—and *come out* with a successful project.

It's simple physics. You can have all the information you want (sourced by waking consciousness) and still have little knowledge (sourced only by the non-conscious). In other words, if you are operating mainly on linearity, you are flying blind.

How then can *this* particular book, which is a linear medium, help? Simply because we are aware of the limitations of linearity and are making you aware of them also, so that together we can get beyond them to the certainty of success. We are insisting on the functions and feeling experience of *non*-linearity.

The overall objective of project management philosophies and methodologies is to *manage and control as much as possible*, since managing and controlling *everything* is not humanly possible.

Since this is done theoretically and as a commodity—that is, as something that needs to apply generically, across the board, to most situations—inevitably many things are missed because in reality, there are no predictable, commoditized projects. **There are only *actual* projects and *hypothesized* methodologies.** How do we breach that gap? How do we get to certainty?

The gap between theory and practice appears every time a project makes itself more and more unique, which means the more involved and longer-lasting, the more changes and surprises and the greater the gap. You get alterations, modifications, new requests, misunderstandings, errors, and all manner of new things popping up. Crisis management then becomes the reality.

We can only breach the gap between *actual* projects and *certainty* by accessing unique elements in the particular project that linearity, threshold skills and hypotheses do *not* have access to, that is, **what the Genius can *capture* that others cannot, what the Genius can *feel* that others do not, what the Genius can *see* that others cannot; *what* the Genius can *know* that others do not**. Those unique elements lead to closing the gap, but they have to be accessed by non-traditional, non-linear means.

That, in sum, is the rationale for **Genius project management**. Geniuses can see beyond linearity to non-linearity. They understand it speaks a different, non-linear language. Geniuses tap volumes of "hidden" knowledge. That knowledge is unique to the Genius Project Manager and his/her situation; it is not available to anyone else. He/she didn't "look it up" somewhere; he/she didn't learn it in school, he/she didn't find it on the dashboard; he didn't Google it; she didn't look to what everyone else is doing or would recommend. They find it inside themselves.

The Genius himself/herself is the only discovery tool for non-linearity, and non-linearity is the key to certainty.

That is "the problem that is not a problem" that people generally have with actual (feeling as) knowledge: that it is held by a *knower*, not by a *server*. How can it be actual knowledge, if no one else can access it digitally? In two ways.

First, the Genius can *lead others to experience* *what he or she is experiencing* (what they *know*), depending on those others' willingness to "see and feel outside the box."

Second, *it makes no difference anyway*, because it's no one else's (damn) business. Geniuses are not at all concerned about what other people think; they lead effectively regardless. They know that other people's vision is extremely limited compared to their own. That's why

Geniuses sometimes seem strange, different, unusual, isolated and even freakish, but that's no one else's (damn) business either!

We won't go into this point in much detail because it's material for a different book on the history of science, but it is useful to mention that what we call "science" consists of culturally accepted—and mandated—knowledge for the masses, *commoditized* knowledge that dismisses *individual* experience and knowledge as "unproven" because it has not received the review and blessing of the scientific establishment. Unproven because there has been no peer review, or control group study. Commoditized knowledge is, as Kuhn called it, "normal science."

In "**The Science Delusion**," by Rupert Sheldrake, we come to one of the most astounding historical ironies in the history of science: *Science is now the Catholic Church*—the same church that Science reacted against with a fierce pursuit and defense of linearity for hundreds of years:

> The biggest scientific delusion of all is that science already knows the answers. The details still need working out, but in principle, the fundamental questions are settled. . . . the belief system that governs conventional scientific thinking is an act of faith, grounded in a nineteenth-century ideology. (pp. 6-7).

> In almost every other sphere of human life, there is not one, but many points of view. There are many languages, cultures, nations, philosophies, religions, sects, political parties, businesses and life-styles. Only in the realm of science can we still find the old ethos of monopoly, universality and

absolute authority that used to be claimed by the Roman Catholic Church. Catholic means 'universal.' At the Reformation, starting in 1517, the Roman Church lost its monopoly; now many other churches and ideologies coexist with it, including atheism. But there is still only one universal science. (p. 326).

Before continuing, be sure you understand the difference between linearity and non-linearity, between in-formation and feeling, and between waking consciousness and the non-conscious mind. None of these concepts are shockingly new; some have been around for over a century (like the concept of the non-conscious mind)—*except for one*: **feeling as knowledge**.

Without feeling, or by avoiding feeling, dismissing feeling, denigrating feeling—the very language of Genius!—any the prescription for Genius will fail. **You cannot rely only on waking consciousness and produce Genius results.** There are endless miles of cemeteries filled with dead projects that testify to this.

That leads us to our second hypothesis:

Hypothesis No. 2: Understanding and accessing *feeling as knowledge* dramatically raises the probability of success in project management for a simple reason: Genius discovers valuable knowledge that there is no other way to get to. That knowledge addresses new issues that come into view and offers exceptional innovations to address them.

This leads us to our third and fourth hypotheses:

Hypothesis No. 3: Continuously successful project management handles *all* the variations, alterations, modifications, and surprises—in short, all the inevitable *unpredictability* of the variations of any project—by means of *Intuition*, which *detects*, and *Innovation*, which *resolves*.

Hypothesis No. 4: <u>Geniuses project managers create Certainty of success</u>, but it isn't created *outside* the Genius. It comes from *inside,* from his/her confidence in having the endless capacity to intuit and to innovate. If you have the self-confidence that you can identify potential problems early on and that you can use them to vault to outstanding solutions that move things forward, then there are no problems.

Innovations are new, useful ideas that are perfect for the situations where they are needed and that come at the right time. Genius identifies most of the issues that would later have become crises. Crises are always the result of things that could not be detected by linear methods, but that were latent and available, but people just don't *know* them. Certainty is *knowing.*

A Brief Word about "Change"

Although we understand the intention behind it, the expression "the only constant is change" doesn't clarify what change actually is. "Change" is an abstract concept. It doesn't mean much except that *there are alterations to what is, that at any given moment, are imminent.*

So what?

If change is a constant, *why are we paying attention to it?* Things that don't change don't need our attention. *Does change itself change?* Does it get faster or slower, or *less "changing"* in any way? Saying that "change is a constant" is clever but says nothing. It's the same as saying, "what is, is." Or that change is predictable. So what?

The real issues about the future and about what you want are *predictability* and *unpredictability.* Predictability is at the heart of our desire for what we call science, knowledge and the scientific method. We use knowledge—or at least we hope to—in order to anticipate how to address situations in our lives and on the planet so that we can get the outcomes we want.

Organizations everywhere use a backwards approach in attempting to build the certainty of successful outcomes. They don't focus on what they actually *want*, they focus much more on the endless fears of "what-might-happen-that-we-*don't-want*, but they aren't really aware of that focus because it has become so habitual. Fear doesn't usually provide solutions.

That focus (drum roll please) *amounts to analyzing a problem* and as we know (see Guideline No. 6 in Part 4), analyzing a problem rather than focusing on the potential solutions and on what *is* working, ends up making the problem *worse* and you probably won't see that coming. You'll be deep into the analysis before you realize, "Wait a minute! This isn't working!"

We are recommending movement in a different direction: *first* figure out what you need/want in order to feel certain and get that feeling in place so that you can see fully what it communicates, *then* move forward.

Don't expect the information hierarchies to handle unpredictability. You need to initiate first, with ideas and feeling, and second, with action, in a different direction.

Why would you act without first getting the knowledge of what's involved in the situation? Yet this is exactly what most people do—"see? I'm doing something to solve it!" Well no, you're actually not, because acting from ignorance ends up being very costly.

One way to establish a basis for solutions is to generate a vision of success with your team, preferably a vision that goes beyond just one individual project, that is based on knowledge/feeling and that sustains team members' aspirations. How far that vision goes ultimately doesn't matter too much, the point of this is to generate energy in a positive direction that engages people that can expand over time that calls on people's best.

Why? Because you cannot de-celerate, eliminate or change a problem, a negative direction, concerns and worries or bad history by studying it, analyzing it or in any way giving it attention and energy. Physics won´t allow it.

Feeling is what gives energy to ideas and thoughts. That's why you cannot analyze or defensively prepare for a problem without making it worse. You won't *see* it happening because waking consciousness doesn't have the bandwidth to reveal the phenomenon. But you can avoid it by directing energy early on and ongoing, in the opposite, *positive* direction of a vision of success that becomes more detailed and whose levels of feeling are deliberately made to expand. Then change will come—the kind of change that you *do* want.

The Vision of Project Success and Feeling It

Geniuses love the feeling they have for their project. That feeling is the essence of their vision of success. It is their organizing principle. Because it is based on feeling, it ensures **leverage** and **coherence.** Leverage means things are made easy; coherence means all the parts work together to create a greater whole than just their sum; they don't fight each other. Linearity cannot do any of this, which is why so many project managers who want coherence and leverage run around hysterically trying to plug all the holes in the dyke, managing by crises.

Non-linearity doesn't take any effort to access consciously, except the ongoing effort to feel good or at least to feel better, to be open and positive, to expect the best. That feeling opens the avenues to the non-conscious mind. Geniuses worry about leverage or coherence; they come naturally in this way.

Remember the experiment where you were listening to a conversation in a busy restaurant or bar? Trying to force waking consciousness to successfully handle a project without deliberately involving the non-conscious mind is like attempting to listen to all the conversations in the bar at the same time. It's just not possible. It's input overload on a system with very limited bandwidth.

You may "multi-task"—a hopelessly mistaken concept—and go from one conversation to another, but your attention will be moving around rather than assimilating everything all at once. Assimilating all at once is exactly what your non-conscious mind does, easily.

Exercising Intuition to *Detect*

Intuition is "gut feel." It is your way of measuring how things are really going, and it's simple: how do you feel, right now, honestly, about how things are going?

You are mainly going to feel one of two ways: either good, because you feel that things are going well, or not-so-good (bad), because things are not going well.

If you feel good, hold that feeling as much as you can. You may be able to identify and appreciate the things you've done, said, felt, generated that get you there and by paying attention to them, you add fuel to them.

If you feel bad, don's start analyzing why but do ask yourself, "what is it, exactly, that doesn't feel so good to me?" There can be a lot of knowledge available in asking that question.

Then, to move yourself in the direction of a solution, ask: "how do I *want* to feel about this situation?" and then ask yourself that question again and again until you can really answer it in detail with a palpable feeling. Not just "I want to feel good," but "I want to be recognized for doing this well," or "I want the conflict to turn into collaboration" or "I want to feel that all is going well and getting better and better," and so on. The words aren't the issue, they are just the container, the structure, to convey the feeling to yourself. There is no energy in words; the energy is always in the feeling behind them.

When you are driving a car, you keep your eyes on the road. When you are addressing your life and work in any way, you keep your awareness on how and what you feel. That does more than keep you from crashing; it keeps you on the road to what you want.

The actual mechanics of exercising Genius:

1. Certainty is a feeling. It is a feeling that you want, because it communicates that you are moving in a direction that you *want* to move in. Things line up.

2. Feelings communicate knowledge on the topic you are focused on; specifically, knowledge about where you stand in the moment and what to do next. If it's negative, then you want to change that feeling because it's only telling you what *not* to do.

3. Feeling can be used to build greater Certainty—the positive feeling you want. Only feeling can create greater feeling, which is to say that only knowledge can create greater knowledge. Which is also to say that you can't create feeling *or* knowledge from just words.

4. To build Certainty, you need to identify what you want, but *at the feeling level*, not just in words. Given our habitual devotion to linearity and words, this takes some practice!

5. Then you need to pursue *that*, internally, as a feeling because that will build inspiration to act in the most useful direction, based on what you really know. You want that inspiration because it is accurate—it is *you*. It is your best guide. You get to feeling good for its own sake, and to get to inspiration (which also feels really good).

6. Once you have that inspiration, then you will know what to do, how to act, what steps to take, what course to follow, what decision to make. Just follow the feeling. It will tell you. Over time, you'll learn to trust how unfailing it is, so experiment if you don't trust it at first.

Innovation is the Heart of Genius Project Management

The problem with the above statement is that the term "innovation" has been thoroughly distorted, defined, and re-defined with subcategories to spare, and rather than generating any clarity all of this has made innovation seem like something arcane, difficult to produce, out of most people's reach, elusive, realistically limited only to small things, requiring all kinds of analysis to produce, based only on "hard work," that can only be done with the direction of experienced senior managers and thus out of most people "league," and ultimately not accessible to us.

People define, redefine, categorize and re-categorize what innovation supposedly is, in the most analytical articles and books that say absolutely nothing about how innovation actually gets generated. Maybe it makes them appear knowledgeable, when they are not.

That is the damage that analyzing innovation has done—mainly, to communicate that to innovate you have to analyze, and that to analyze you have to choose a category of innovation first. This is all just grade A baloney. We won't go into all the historical reasons why all this baloney has been generated over the years, but there you have it.

The most important things to know about innovation are that,

> **1.) It is easy and is a normal human capability that anyone can exercise;**

> **2.) It doesn't require analysis of *any* kind in order to be produced; and**

3.) It's simple. Innovation is just a new exceptional idea at the right time, for the right situation.

You don't have to analyze for that either. If someone tells you that innovation is hard, or that in order to innovate you first have to analyze whatever, head for the door. Yell, "Check please!"

You already know all the things that people who produce mediocre projects believe, because those are all the *threshold requirements* you already know about, plus—lest we forget— the proverbial "hard work." Geniuses don't have much patience for giving importance to any of that because none of those are in any way related to superior results.

Project management IS about approaching each situation as if it were the first time, for the novelty and the pleasure of discovery and creating something new. It's about coming up with more efficient (and even more enjoyable) ways of doing things. Project management is about co-creation, learning with other people, how to improve how things are done. Project management is about coming up with new, unexpected, expansive perspectives about the project, about the team, about stakeholders... Project management is about leading a passionate, idea-generating group of people. Project management is about the pleasure of newness, of differentness, of discovery. Project management is about creation.

Waking consciousness does not innovate anything at all, ever. Waking consciousness does not have the bandwidth capacity to create solutions. It only makes you *think* that it does. Waking consciousness performs one fundamental task—a task so fundamental it is ingrained in our behavior and we don't notice it: *it allows us to choose what we want, continuously*: preferences, aspirations, hopes, dreams, likes, wants, desires, selections—are all squarely in the domain of waking consciousness. From there, the *non*-conscious mind takes over if we let it.

Tor Nørretranders summarizes this in **"The User Illusion, Cutting Consciousness Down to Size"** (see sidebar). He refers to waking consciousness as the "I" awareness, and the non-conscious mind as the "Me":

> This distinction between an *I* and a *Me* is considerably less "innocent" than it sounds. It summarizes **the radical changes in perception of what it means to be human that are emerging at the end of the twentieth century**: People are not conscious of very much of what they sense; people are not conscious of very much of what they think; people are not conscious of very much of what they do.
>
> **Man is not primarily conscious. Man is primarily nonconscious**. The idea of a conscious *I* as a housekeeper of everything that comes in and goes out of one is an illusion; perhaps a useful one, but still an illusion. (p. 269). [Boldface ours.]

He is describing what Julian Jaynes already told us, except that when he wrote it, Jaynes did not have the benefit we have today (and that Norretranders has) of technologies that can examine the brain's functioning in extraordinary, new ways.

Despite the fact that we know, with proven scientific evidence in brain neurology that has existed for some time, we still search for solutions and innovations using waking consciousness as our primary tool—all destined to abject failure.

Given our love of immediate cause-and-effect and linearity, there are hundreds and hundreds of innovation "solutions" proffered on sites like youtube.com, linkedin.com, and many others, promising that if you follow the processes that only *they* can provide—then and only then—will you be able to innovate. Baloney.

First they make the point that "innovation is difficult," which is not true, but necessary to rein you in. If you don't know that only the *non*-conscious mind can innovate—which incidentally they don't know either, judging from their Rube Goldberg-esque "solutions" they offer, then you can easily fall into the trap of thinking that innovation *is* difficult. We recall one website that pronounced, "You have to try over 100 times to get to an innovation!" Well, 100 times of what? And why 100, and not 99 or 76?

Anyone who tells you that innovation is difficult is trying to sell you something. Next they'll say they have a special formula, or a unique "pipeline" . . .

Innovation *is* easy—it's human nature. Ask any social psychologist: it's called the Achievement drive. Everyone has it to some degree. It's been documented and researched to death (mainly since the 1960's, especially by the late Prof. David C. McClelland of Harvard University. See his book, **"The Achieving Society"** 1967).

Innovation only requires what you already know. Anyone who has difficulty with innovation isn't listening to their *own* voice, which is the single, most fundamental requirement of Genius.

"Pipelines" do not create innovations because innovations aren't commodities and aren't produced by machines or systems. Innovations are ultimately the product of a mind (and minds) of Genius and are thus tied to that Genius' (those Genius') essential, intimate identities and aspirations. There are no innovations that did not originate in the aspirations and identity of individual minds. That's why there is no software that can crank out an innovation. Software doesn't speak the language; it can't *feel* its way there.

It's not, as many would have you believe, just a question of coming up with "new ideas." You can come up with hundreds and hundreds of new ideas and none of them will fit the intricately networked context that spells success for a particular situation and person(s).

Brainstorming is a waste of brains. Those ideas are throw-aways. How does the non-conscious mind ever get to know the particular, intricate context that can lead to astounding success? Who cares?

You *can* come up with "improvements" to what already exists, but improvements are not innovations. That's why many organizations have tacitly given up on innovation altogether. As the Harvard Business Review put it recently: **"Despite massive investments of management and time and money, innovation remains a frustrating pursuit in many companies."** [June, 2015].

Or as we prefer to put it: **you can't "think outside the box" when your thinking *is* the box.**

The Paradox of Innovation

The major cause of problems we have with innovation today is that we think of it as "disruptive." It became more difficult for *anyone* to innovate when we started thinking of it in that way. It gave us the illusion that there is a stability of some kind that exists prior to innovations making an appearance and disrupting everything.

For something to be disruptive, there has to be something that gets disrupted. We assume that what gets disrupted is something external, like customer markets, existing products, entire industries, an organization's identity, existing strategy, the project plan, and so on. That "something" that gets disrupted is, in contrast to the disruption, *stable, predictable, calm, solid, unchanging, free of interference, safe, certain, reliable, reassuring.* You can't have a disruption without there being an *"un*disrupted."

But there is nothing external to any business that is any of those things—stable, calm, predictable—ever. **There is nothing external to us that is, of itself, certain or safe or reliable**. It's only our blindness to what is already happening continuously, that makes us think external entities, organizations, products, markets, or plans are stable, safe or certain. Plenty of things can be "disruptive;" **what is new about the innovation that makes its appearance isn't that it's disruptive**. We'll get to what it is. And by the way, being "disruptive" is an effect. It's not a cause!

"Disruptive" characterizes the existence of any entity, organic or not, on this planet including the planet itself. Things are disrupted all the time. Our usual focus, however, isn't on change or disruption, it's on thinking that things are "under control" and stable when they really aren't. Our idea of control is distorted and primitive; so is our ability to produce innovations.

An innovation is *the right, great, new idea or solution at the right time.* Innovations are idiosyncratic and circumstantial. They aren't "disruptive" in a universe where nothing is stable; they are really just more of the same. Things are stable *enough* so that we can see that they aren't stable at all.

Without *any* stability at all there would be no change at all—one requires the other, like darkness requires light. If we didn't have the concept of light, we wouldn't have the concept of darkness. **Meaning comes from contrast.** We have just enough stability for us to know that there is change and "disruption," but not so much that nothing changes. Disruption itself isn't what brings innovations to light, or what makes us notice and care about them. Disruption is just an adjective that explains the past; it tells us nothing about what is new. **Innovations are about the future.**

Innovations aren't disruptive, they are revealing and illuminating. What innovations reveal and illuminate is the (possible) future. This is not a minor, semantic point; it goes to the essence of *what* innovations are and *how* they are produced.

Innovation doesn't come from externals. Something new and extraordinary doesn't just suddenly make an appearance out of nowhere.

What is superior performance in project management?

Since on the face of it, projects are eminently linear, it would seem that project managers who are most solidly linear thinkers, who most espouse linear processes and measurements, would be the most successful. That wouldn't be difficult to identify, except that since linearity is the valued language, you may have Genius project managers who disguise themselves by only acknowledging linearity in their conversations. Who want to go out on a limb if you don't have to?

Linearity must be a part of all project planning. The activities or tasks involved are fragments that have to be lined up in the right sequence to produce the desired outcomes. It's just not enough to ensure success.

Many are the projects that have failed spectacularly, that will dutifully tracked on project software, that had "dashboards" and all manner of progress indicators, that met their milestones, there were signed off as complete in each of their stages, that stayed within their budgets, that hit their numbers, that never veered "off track." Inexperienced project managers think that the key to project planning is to master linearity. That is not true at all. Linearity is only a *threshold skill* for project planning.

What is a threshold skill? It's a concept that was developed by social psychologists during the 1970's. It means a skill that is needed for the job but that is an entry-level requirement and not evidence of superior performance. **Threshold skills do not distinguish between superior-performance and average performance in a given job, no matter how good you are at them.**

Linearity, as a threshold skill, has nothing to do with distinguishing between superior-performing project managers and average-performing project managers. If you don't understand linearity and linear resources like project-planning software, you won't get hired and/or could get fired, but you won't produce Genius performance either.

Threshold skills are very easy to detect in a hiring process because they can be measured, often in numbers. Years on the job? Number of projects managed? Within budget? On time? People managed? Total dollars invested? And so on.

You certainly wouldn't want to hire someone primarily because they're good at budgets and math, for example. Handling budgets effectively is a threshold skill for project managers: you need to understand how to use them, but being particularly good at them isn't going to make you a superior-performing project manager.

You're not going to get a promotion or a bonus because you're good at linear thinking. The difference is elsewhere. In fact, if you ignore the language of Genius your projects will most likely get into trouble.

In the period between the 1970's to the 1990's, many jobs were studied for what then was called "job competence," which means something different than what the term "competence" degenerated into. Its current meaning actually means threshold skills. You are competent if you can carry out the job, and today's "competency models" are models for mediocre performance.

Why is this so and what are the implications?
In the history of business intelligence and academic studies of business success, we go all the way back to Frederick Taylor (1856-1915) and his so-called "scientific management." It was a great success at the time and even

inspired the creation of business schools that today, if they fully accepted the historical truths involved, might be seriously embarrassed as a result.

Taylor was a dedicated researcher of measurement, not of science, but he equated the two. He established and proved no hypothesis at all except, possibly, "working harder produces more work." The most intelligent and detailed assessment of Taylor and his work can be found in Matthew Stewart's very engaging book, "The Management Myth":

What we're pointing out is the slavish dedication to measurement, so much so that it was identified with "being scientific." Taylor's "scientific management," despite what were certainly his best intentions, had plenty of linearity but no science.

His work did, however, unleash all manner of studies and theories based on linear methods, for assessing and hiring potential candidates for jobs. In the mid to late 20th century however, we discovered—through seriously scientific methods with defined hypotheses, published methodologies, shared studies and carefully selected control groups—that any rigorous study of the thinking and acting that generates superior performance in almost any job including a great variety of management jobs, is based on what today would be called varieties of "emotional intelligence."

In other words, it is only the distinctly *non*-linear capabilities that reliably distinguish superior performance. If you can easily measure the performance characteristics, to rank the candidates you are considering, then they probably do not measure their probabilities for superior performance in the job.

What characteristics do predict superior performance in the project manager job? It is the characteristics that show evidence that the individual has some of the Genius abilities we are addressing in this book: that he or she can perceive from the environment what others do not; that he or she can understand and decipher what those perceptions mean; that he or she can think like a Genius in determining what is to be done about them, and so on.

The Commoditization of YOU

Commoditization has always been at the heart of the Industrial Age and now, further refined and practically enshrined into religion, it is at the heart of the Information Age which has accelerated it into a hyper-speed. It is, however, invisible to almost everyone because the alternative is invisible. Without contrast you are effectively blind.

We have explained how the assembly-line was conceived of and composed of fragments arranged in a sequence that must be followed for it to make sense, that is, to produce what it is supposed to produce. This was of course understood even earlier than the Gutenberg's printing press assembly-line. Gutenberg's own genius was to create moveable type, which enabled that assembly-line to produce a great variety of products that could be configured easily and quickly.

That assembly-line was language-based and so were all of its products, ultimately contributing to near-universal literacy. Literacy is at the heart of what we typically think of as linearity—one thing after another, all lined up like the letters in a word, in order to *make sense*. So much so that many people think that you can't think without words which is a testament to how far we have come, in our distorted de-humanization of turning who we really are into commodities.

Yes, commoditization is wonderful, and the possibilities of making innovations and solutions easily available to millions are wonderful, with the exception that they end up—if we consider commoditization the end-all—diminishing our capacity to innovate and solve problems in the first place. Historically, this has been happening quickly.

What is that based on? Well, simply that most people and certainly most people organized into business enterprises, seem to think that a perfectly normal and easy human function like achievement and innovation are difficult. If you step back and consider this from a non-linear perspective, you can appreciate how non-sensical that is. People are really *designed* to invent, to come up with ideas, to feel their way to the new, to innovate, to go past what has been achieved before, to improve, to supersede, to ignite the new, to uproot and replace the old...

"Commoditization," as both a *value* and a *belief*, is responsible for this in the Information Age. The accomplishments of the linear mindset seem formidable. Conceptually, however, they are mired in a rigid materialist thinking and prolong a cultural infancy based on learning how to read and write, now extended into learning words for categories of things we hadn't considered.

As we have mentioned, linearity has a profound love for categorization. Categorization provides the illusion of conceptual accomplishment, even of discovery although it mostly leads nowhere. It gives us the hope that the flood of information can somehow be stemmed, even controlled. The entire field of what is called "knowledge management" is mainly based on categorization, yet it misses the most important category of all that it professes to master, despite its name—that of knowledge, which it is fundamentally clueless about.

It's reminiscent of García Márquez's primitive, country village of Macondo in **"One Hundred Years of Solitude,"** where "The world was so recent that many things lacked a name and to mention them, you had to point them out with your finger." And so we have not just innovation, but *disruptive* innovation and *continuous* innovation. That has been around for a number of years. Others have attempted further classifications of it and additional nomenclature. Recently a prominent business journal published a scholarly article with another half-dozen categories for innovation.

Does any of this categorization make it easier in any way at all, to actually *produce* an innovation? Of course not. When linearity wants to exercise itself, it creates categories for the illusion of motion forward, the illusion of control, the illusion of capability. Still, it ends up nowhere except filling more scholarly articles with debates and nomenclature.

These illusions are at the heart of most analysis. Analysis is based on fragmentation, one of the two primary characteristics of linearity (the other is sequencing). Analysis takes things or ideas apart, ostensibly to better understand them. Once they are fragmented and classified, they can be easily documented in languages and thus, stored, edited or transported.

Analysis is the principal effort involved in problem-solving, although of itself, it provides absolutely no solutions at all and in most cases expands the problem itself. With this expansion of the problem, those who are attempting to solve it feel like they are really onto something useful—now we know something we didn't know before. Not really. Now you've created another aspect of the problem you didn't have to deal with before.

The primary functions of waking consciousness, so limited yet so very agile, are first, to *focus* and in focusing, to choose; and second, to create illusions. The primary illusion of waking consciousness is always to have us believe that it sees much more than it does. It wants to *be* the non-conscious!

The Information Age—from Gutenberg forward—fundamentally changed innovation in at least two major ways. It made innovation easier to educate people in, and it focused innovation on commoditization *first*, too early on to let ideas breathe and expand and mutate to greater maturity. Linearity loves beginnings. Those illusions are not malicious; they are the result of being able to focus. The non-conscious mind cannot do that.

A venture capitalist wants to know not only that you have a good idea, but that the idea is *scalable*. Scalability refers to the ability to make the idea a *bone fide* commodity that succeeds at the balancing act of being *unique*—irreproducible in the sense that it can't be easily copied—and *easy to copy*, in the sense that millions (in both senses of that term) can be produced.

Notice how insistently marketers attempt to make their products appear to be easily customized, unique or somehow perfectly made for *you*. They are fighting the inevitable: that their scalable product is "one size fits all." That's not necessarily a bad thing, but with some products it's a serious cost issue.

Commoditization as a process is the opposite of Genius. Culturally and especially in education, the commoditization of ideas and information and especially the denial and ignorance regarding knowledge means that for most people, Genius practically doesn't exist.

Educational systems are based on commoditization. One size, or just a few sizes, fit most if not all. An equally strong force has been the rise of so-called Knowledge Management, which has little to do with management and nothing to do with knowledge. Knowledge Management is the "industrial" response in support of the digital age; it was inevitable although non-sensical—just as non-sensical yet timely in its marketing savvy as Frederick Taylor's "scientific management," which had little to do with management and nothing to do with science (but everything to do with *measurement*. Measurement, of itself, is not science.)

The only way you can recognize Genius, which no one seems to these days because it seems so scarce and so impossible to identify clearly, is if you abandon the idea that information and knowledge are the same thing, and that *human knowing is unique in each individual*. That's were Genius resides, in that uniqueness.

Yes, we know that all "Knowledge Management" articles and books attempt to distinguish between *information* and *knowledge*, making it clear that what the authors offer isn't merely ways to control information—which is exactly what it really is—but rather, something more rarified, more exalted that only they can really decipher.

KM does not distinguish at all between information and knowledge, and this distinction is important because it exists as a fundamental, distinguishing part of human realities. KM offers circular and/or convoluted definitions in its semantic gymnastics for attempting to separate ("categorize") the two. "Knowledge is information that..." Etc. No, no, no. knowledge is not information. Information is data, *in formation*. It sits in a server. Knowledge is what can be produced and held by a *knower*. It is *non*-linear, unlike in-formation. **Feeling is knowledge.**

It is difficult to underestimate the distorted effects in our thinking caused by our historic, millennial disparagement and rejection of *human feeling*. Most people think of it as thinking, not as feeling. Denunciations of "positive thinking," for example, cross that line and back all the time. Thinking and feeling are different, although both can involve ideas. Consider the difference between when you *think* you know something, and when you *know* that you know it.

We value commoditization greatly without also appreciating what we call idiosyncrasy, that is, a characteristic that is unique to an individual. The most disparaging term that is applied to idiosyncratic people, people we would define as those who know who they really are and are fully, unabashedly *themselves*, is when they are called *freaks*. Let's be clear. In order to become a Genius you need to reconcile yourself with the fact that you *are* a "freak" and that this is the single greatest thing about you.

No one else has your perspective on life. No one else has your experiences, your particular beliefs and the conclusions you have made about what you want from life. In addition, no one else can support, energize and accelerate your own dreams for you. Ultimately, only you are responsible for them. They are what most easily characterizes and defines your particular Genius.

Genius is finally not about listening to advice or suggestions or expectations other people may have for you, and they will have many, most especially those that haven't come anywhere near their own dreams. There is one voice for you to hear above all others and that is your own. As one of us put it in an article titled "The End of Teaching and Training,"

> Anyone who tells you that innovation is difficult is trying to sell you something. Next they'll say they have a special formula, or a unique "pipeline" . . .
> Innovation *is* easy—it's human nature. Ask any social psychologist: it's called the Achievement drive. Everyone has it to some degree. It only requires what you already know. Anyone who has difficulty with innovation isn't listening to their *own*

voice, which is the single, most fundamental requirement of genius.

As you are coming to know, that voice doesn't speak in linear terms. Linearity is conventionality and leads mostly to mediocrity. Genius comes from *feeling:* imagination, intuition, insight, introspection...

Genius project management means that ephemeral, distorted or potentially negative information won't affect you much at all, because beyond information there is knowledge. That is why Geniuses consider information and why for Genius project managers, information is useful but it is rarely important. Knowledge is very important. It's the difference between receiving piecemeal bits of reality one after another, like crumbs along a long path, versus receiving a whole, integrated picture.

Why Genius is Possible in the Universe

Genius is possible in the universe only because of one reason: Genius is possible because the knowledge, experiences and feeling of each individual are completely idiosyncratic, that is, **no one else can ever *know* what you *know*; no one else can ever *experience* what you *experience*; no one else can ever *feel* what you *feel*.**

They can think they can and often may; they may believe that because their circumstances seem similar, that so is what they feel. All that similarity is entirely made up.

The Vision of Infinite Success

The vision of success that Genius project managers hold is not short-term and is certainly not limited to one project. Genius project managers are focused on being true to the identity they aspire to and that is not a short-term objective.

As a consequence, their concept of success is not contingent on one project. The current project is part of a larger view of success which is not dependent on specific projects, but rather on a broad view of mastering their craft, of understanding how to develop *knowledge as feeling*.

We are using terminology along the lines of what James P. Carse talks about in his brilliant book, titled "Finite and Infinite Game, A Vision of Life as Play and Possibility." If feeling good is how to unlock the doorway to the non-conscious mind, then play is its supreme unfolding.

Finite games like the typical project, are carried out primarily to be won, which is when the objectives are accomplished within the constraints that were expected: time and money. Infinite games are how Geniuses view project management, even though they play the finite game of individual projects. Vision is different in each.

Finite games are singular, are played win/lose, and have boundaries that are well-defined in advance. As James Carse puts it,

> A boundary is a phenomenon of opposition. It is the meeting place of hostile forces. Where nothing opposes, there can be no boundary. One cannot move beyond a boundary without being resisted. (Carse, p. 69).

Infinite games, however, aren't bounded by visionary and thus seeing only horizons. The infinite game is the very life and identity of the Genius manager that is the *infinite player*. Finite players are playing to win in the immediate, short term. Infinite players have a different definition of play and are looking not to *end* but to *continue* the play.

> A horizon is a phenomenon of vision. One cannot look at the horizon; it is simply the point beyond which we cannot see. There is nothing in the horizon itself, however, that limits vision, for the horizon opens onto all that lies beyond itself. What limits vision is rather the incompleteness of that vision.
> One never reaches a horizon. It is not a line; it has no place; it encloses no field; its location is always relative to the view. To move toward a horizon is simply to have a new horizon. . . .
> Every move an infinite player makes is toward the horizon. Every move made by a finite player is within a boundary (Carse, p. 70).

Perspective is everything. Perspective is especially useful in understanding and transforming "bad" situations or "bad" feelings. We live in a reality of frameworks that drive how we interpret everything. Those frameworks are beliefs. When our beliefs no longer serve us because we are attempting to go beyond them, something crashes. Those crashes are seen as disasters in the short term. The bigger perspective, however, comes from the Genius that we really are. The perspective always offers relief.

Intuition
Acting Can Be a Huge Waste of Time

In order to be a Genius project manager, you'll need to make peace with and develop your capacity to enjoy *thinking*. Geniuses know that Western culture's historic mad rush to always *act before thinking* wastes time, energy and opportunities. Anywhere you go, successful people will tell you to *act*. Millionaire entrepreneurs will encourage immediate, continuous, passionate *action*. Self-help books, videos and video clips wax over and over on the importance of *acting*.

Acting before thinking, or more specifically, acting without addressing your own *feeling* (knowledge) far in advance of action, is one of the many mistaken things we teach ourselves. This is what we call *the shotgun approach* to success: just act out all over the place and *something's* bound to work. We could show you video after video, book quote after book quote, extolling the importance of acting to achieve success in pretty much anything, but you won't have to long hard if you want to see what we're talking about. In fact, you probably already know this. In sum, acting for the sake of exerting yourself is acting without knowing. Acting without knowing is, frankly, stupid.

Geniuses seem to know this. Thinking and feeling are vitally important to Geniuses because everything else, including any action they come up with, are secondary to thinking and feeling.

For many people acting is a corollary of the Protestant Ethic, or if not that particular organized religion, some other that insists that human beings are somehow unworthy, not good enough, or have to do a variety of things "correctly" in order to be deserving—and religions always manage to come up with a host of things you supposedly need to do. "Workaholics" are highly esteemed. No matter how much we may insist that we or others should "work smarter, not harder," we generally don't believe that at all. Workaholics are virtuous, they are admired, they are hired and promoted... even though frankly, they usually aren't very bright—with one exception that we'll get to.

If this is part of your belief system, and undoubtedly so some degree or another it has been, then there are beliefs you will need to examine and in this section will explain how to identify and change beliefs.

In sum, if being a man or woman of *action* is more important to you, then you probably will not focus on thinking and feeling as much as Geniuses need to. You will also probably need more rest and sleep to recover from your overwork.

As a Genius, you'll need to identify what it is about thinking and feeling that you like, and this book will give you plenty of things to choose from. Thinking and feeling are natural, normal and unavoidable for human beings, but we are talking about *deliberate* thinking and feeling, not the kind that are targeted at you by the Information Age: social media, news media, entertainment media, work-place media, and almost any communication with friends, family and other people. As a Genius, you'll begin to discern where and how to spend your time.

A good rule for Geniuses is MYOB. Mind your own business. Everyone else is just passing the time. People get into other people's business because they've given up on their own dreams.

Technology trains us to *notice* and to *react* but not to *know*. The capacity for intimacy and the possibilities for knowledge diminish, the more information we pay attention to. Waking consciousness doesn't have the bandwidth to handle both information and knowledge at the same time.

In **"The User Illusion,"** author Norretranders quotes (1965) from Dietrick Trincker, a German physiologist:

> "'Of all the information that every second flows into our brains from our sensory organs, only a fraction arrives in our consciousness: the *ratio* of the capacity of *perception* to the capacity of *apperception* is at best a million to one,' . . . 'That is to say, only *one millionth* of what our eyes see, our ears hear, and our other senses inform us about *appears in our consciousness.*'"

It is a surprising effect of the Information Age that it moves us *away* from knowledge *towards* information and reaction. Innovation and Genius project management are about *knowing*, not about being informed. You really have to be deliberate if you want to *know*.

And so, we go back to our fundamental definition: *feeling is knowledge*. Everything else is linear. Everything else is information. Everything else is data*, in formation.*

We all speak linear languages. The natural, spoken language we learned when we were children, and we may have learned more than one of these. Then there is also the language(s) of mathematics. We may know some computer programming languages. We may know languages from many other sources like video games or the arts.

Then there is the non-linear language of feeling that we all use, all the time. We may not appreciate it or understand how to use it, but if you are human you will feel unless you are taking deliberate measures to numb yourself. Not all of these measures need to be chemical, either; there are negative beliefs about feeling that over time, can end up numbing you.

There are two primary questions for accessing what you feel:

> What do I want in this moment?
> What do I feel in this moment?

Geniuses, the Finite Game and the Infinite Game

Geniuses don't see the project they are currently managing as the be-all and end-all, which most people do when they define their well-being and their lives around their work or their career. Linear thinking is big on endings.

Linear thinking needs to define an end, despite its unavoidable incompleteness. If you define yourself and your identity on a single project, then you risk everything. Mentally pursuing one project is a finite game. It is an exercise, however long it may last, that will end one way or another. No matter how well it ends, you will move on because life always moves on. At the end of any project, no matter how poorly it may have ended, you may not realize it but *you* are "new and improved." Geniuses know to look for this in themselves, regardless of other people's standards or opinions.

The "infinite game" that Geniuses know they are playing is the game of expanding their own burgeoning, creative identity. Who you are becoming doesn't end, like projects do. Geniuses play for the long term because big dreams, whatever they may be, offer endless opportunities for discovery, creativity and for the expansion of who they really are (becoming). *That's* what Geniuses want, not merely to have projects become a great success. They aren't playing just to win the *finite* game; they are playing to enjoy and extend the enjoyment of the *infinite* game. The first is played for winning (up to a point); the second is played for the pleasure if creation.

Look around you. Almost everyone is playing a very finite project management game. They are focused on the short-term; they believe that linear project indicators (budget, time-frames) are not only a "reality" but the *only* reality; they are only satisfied by immediate cause-and-effect and so are often impatient and controlling; they assign blame because their picture of reality is so small, which is how they ultimately see their own influence; they see their own identity as unchanging; they pay more attention to what other people think that to what they themselves feel...

The infinite project manager is playing for the long-term—not the long-term for the company, client, project or job, but for the long term of his/her own identity and future life. They understand and deliberately use the complexities of long-term causes and effects; they can't assign blame because to them, it feels like giving away something valuable. They see their own identity expanding in exciting ways; and they pay no attention to what other people may think, but lots of attention to how they themselves are feeling.

Perspective is everything. When you play the game of life from the perspective of an infinite game, then the nature of "negativity" or "losing" changes completely. You cannot lose if the "game" doesn't end.

You especially cannot lose if you understand that failure is actually an opportunity you haven't yet seen clearly. Geniuses look for and identify the hidden challenge in any "negative" outcomes. That challenge is an opportunity to extend their mastery of the language of the non-conscious. It is an opportunity for them to become bigger. For the Genius, these aren't just words. They are a vital *feeling* they pursue. As Carse puts it:

> Finite players play within boundaries; infinite players play with boundaries. (Carse, p. 12).

Bibliography

The following lists books that are mainly cited or referenced in the text.
It is not an inventory of the research carried out for this book.

Andreasen, Nancy C.; "**The Creating Brain, The Neuroscience of Genius**," Dana Press, New York, N.Y., 2005.

Bohm, David, and Peat, F. David; "**Science, Order, and Creativity, A Dramatic New Look at the Creative Roots of Science and Life**,' Bantam, New York, N.Y., 1987.

Boyatzis, Richard; "**The Competent Manager, A Model for Effective Performance**," John Wiley & Sons, New York, N.Y., 1982.

Carse, James P.; "**Finite and Infinite Games, A Vision of Life as Play and Possibility**," Ballantine Books, New York, N.Y., 1986.

Damasio, Antonio; "**Self Comes to Mind, Constructing the Conscious Brain**," Vintage Books, New York, N.Y., 2012.

"**Descartes' Error: Emotion, Reason, and the Human Brain**," Vintage, New York, N.Y., 2006.

"**The Feeling of What Happens: Body and Emotion in the Making of Consciousness**,"Harcourt, Brace & Co., Orlando, FL, 1999.

"**Looking for Spinoza: Joy, Sorrow, and the Feeling Brain**," Harcourt, Inc., Orlando, FL, 2003.

"Self Comes to Mind, Constructing the Conscious Brain," Vintage Books, New York, N.Y., 2012.

Floridi, Luciano; "Information, A Very Short Introduction," Oxford University Press, New York, N.Y., 2010.

Gilligan, Carol; "In a Different Voice, Psychological Theory and Women's Development," Harvard U. Press, Cambridge, MA, 1982.

Goleman, Daniel; Boyatzis, Richard; McKee, Annie; "Primal Leadership, Realizing the Power of Emotional Intelligence," Harvard Business School Publishing, Boston, MA, 2002.

Greenspan, Stanley I., M.D. and Shanker, Stuart G., D. Phil.; "The First Idea, How Symbols, Language, and Intelligence Evolved From Our Primate Ancestors to Modern Humans;" Da Capo Press, Cambridge, MA, 2004.

Jaynes, Julian; "The Origin of Consciousness in the Breakdown of the Bicameral Mind," Mariner Books, New York, N.Y., 2000.

Kline, Morris; "Mathematics, the Loss of Certainty," Oxford University Press, New York, N.Y., 1980.

Kuhn, Thomas S.; "The Structure of Scientific Revolutions," 3rd edition, University of Chicago Press, London, 1996.

Lakoff, George, and Núñez, Rafael E.; "Where Mathematics Comes From, How the Embodied Mind Brings Mathematics Into Being; Basic Books, New York, N.Y., 2000.

Lewis, Marc; "The Biology of Desire, Why Addiction Is Not a Disease," Perseus, New York, N.Y., 2015.

Lukacs, John; **"At the End of an Age,"** Yale U. Press, New Haven, CT, 2002.

McLuhan, Marshall, and Fiore, Quentin; **"War and Peace in the Global Village,"** Hardwired, San Francisco, CA, 1968.

 "The Gutenberg Galaxy, The Making of Typographic Man," University of Toronto Press, Toronto, Canada, 1962.

 "The Medium is the Massage, An Inventory of Effects," Gingko Press, Corte Madera, CA, 1967.

Nørretranders, Tor; "The **User Illusion, Cutting Consciousness Down to Size,"** Penguin, New York, N.Y., 1998.

Schwart, Jeffrey M., M.D. and Begley, Sharon **"The Mind and the Brain, Neuroplasticity and the Power of Mental Force,"** Harper Collins, New York, N.Y., 2002.

Sheldrake, Rupert; **"A New Science of Life, The Hypothesis of Morphic Resonance,"** Park Street Press, Rochester, VT, 1995.

 "The Science Delusion," Hodder & Stoughton, Ltd., London, 2013.

Shorto, Russell; **"Descartes' Bones, A Skeletal History of the Conflict Between Faith and Reason;** Doubleday, New York, N.Y., 2008.

Stewart, Mattew; **"The Management Myth, Why the Experts Keep Getting It Wrong,"** W. W. Norton & Co., New York, N.Y., 2009.

About the Authors

As a project manager Jorge Escotto has over fifteen years of experience working for Fortune 500 corporations, and personally executed hundreds of projects in 25 countries in that capacity. He has two PMI® certifications including PMP® and PMI-RMP®, and has a master of Information Technology.

None of that is what ultimately made him perfect for co-authoring this book, however. It was necessary first, that he completely master and succeed internationally (and cross-culturally) as a project manager, in order to then be able to identify the exact, massive and subtle limitations of all *linear formats, protocols and recommendations*. He can directly connect what they aspire to but then fail to produce as a consequence of their linearity.

He has an exceptional eye for this. José Santiago Pedrosa discovered in Jorge a stunning, prescient understanding of the boundaries implicit in those formats and protocols—an understanding so second-nature it is seldom identified or articulated by anyone. In that way, Jorge served as the perfect diagnostician, sounding board, inspiration and innovator for what this book presents and was essential to its creation. If Geniuses can readily see beyond the appearances of things—and we know that they can—then his career is a perfect example of that capacity.

What is least interesting about Jose Santiago is he's 35 years working with technology in four continents. What is most interesting is what he was reading between the lines during that time about human brain neurology.